A Call for Inspection Unit for Research Students' Supervision

Elizabeth Paradiso Urassa

Published by Information is Power, 2023.

Also by Elizabeth Paradiso Urassa

Strategies to Overcome Challenges in Academic Supervision
Simple and Silly Social -Cultural Strategies to Fight Isolation in Higher
Education
The Academic Support Research Students Must Obtain from Supervisors
Articulating Research Students' Relational and Social Expectations
A Call for Inspection Unit for Research Students' Supervision

Table of Contents

This book is for all higher education stakeholders who desire change in research students' supervision and are for students' retention and graduation.

A CALL FOR INSPECTION UNIT FOR RESEARCH STUDENTS' SUPERVISION

The Crying voices of University Research Students Worldwide

Thank you for choosing this

BOOK

You are the voice we need

for supervision reformation

in higher education

Definition of Terms

Partners Mainly refer to students and supervisors in postsecondary education who collaborate in research learning.

Learning aids All sorts of materials teachers and students employ in their learning settings facilitate understanding of the intended learning contents. They may include but are not limited to visualizing items such as charts, diagrams, chemicals, apparatuses, or audio such as cassettes, DVDs, CDs, and digital video.

Learning agencies All support students academically and socially, including supervisors, librarians, and (laboratory/computer) technicians.

Supervisor A university teacher responsible for teaching, guiding, and instructing research students concerning their projects. It is used interchangeably with teachers, academics, faculty, and scholars.

Inspection Is a process of monitoring and examining the activities and cooperation of learning participants, mainly supervisors, and students.

School inspection The practice of listening, observing, recording, conversing, and reporting the school practices, including students' learning sessions. It includes examining all learning activities and relationships between learners, school leadership, and teachers. The process includes exploring learning resources in a school and reporting the situation to the responsible contextual organ, sometimes without providing expert advice.

Supervision Implies the revolution of school inspection in secondary schools and refers to the individual learning process where the supervisor directs, oversees, and guides research students in postsecondary education.

Higher education (HE) stakeholders - All individuals interested in and influencing the postsecondary learning and teaching process. In addition, people and organs affect resource allocation and other practices in HE; thus, students, parents, donors, governments, institutions, teachers, and families are in this category.

List of Tables

6

List of Figures

Acknowledgement

I thank all who contribute with their stories and allow me to share them in this book. The informants are many, and writing their names in this book may take five pages. Unfortunately, some narratives are not included even though they were relevant due to the limitation I set for myself concerning the page number of this book. I might use the stories in another related book under the consent of the informers. Therefore, if you read and see that the story you shared is not written in this book, do not despair; another book is on its way.

I want to thank Prof. Isaksen and Espen for their constructive advice. Likewise, I thank the doctoral student who provided the email for discussion in this book. I am also grateful to the department head for permission to publicly discuss her response to the student's complaint. I know she did not know better, but she might have seen the need to establish an independent unit in her institution. I hope she has regretted her biased judgment and that she desires experts to deal with disputes in the supervision of research students objectively. In addition, I want to encourage people who have withdrawn from higher education due to failure in supervision to air their voices. It is healthy to talk about it until we see the required changes because supervision of research degree students is the foundation of learning in postsecondary education. We all need to be safe when we consult teachers and trust their guidance, but if we fear and think they are dream killers, it will hinder us from working with them effectively.

Finally, I thank my family members and children for their support. Be blessed all days of your lives

Introduction

Higher education (HE) learning is undoubtedly calamitous; thus, research students' supervision needs reform. Currently, students in most higher education institutions (HEIs) depend on individual learning led by their supervisors. The supervisors support students with planning, strategizing, and evaluating the learning process and outcomes. Unfortunately, in most cases, the current supervision system favors supervisors, and that has been the cause of student attrition in many universities. Scholarly literature informs the challenges and complexity surrounding higher education learning rooted in supervision failure, but little has been done to rectify the situation. Likewise, scholars have indicated the difficulty of supervising students and the factors affecting students and supervisors in their cooperation that need attention.

Regrettably, the scholars' discussions, research findings, and debates have not changed the situation because still, students drop out caused of challenges in supervision persist in many countries. Indeed, the problems related to supervision have become a stumbling block for many students, hindering them from attaining their learning goals and graduating. Surprisingly, no one has thought of having an independent unit for supervision monitoring and evaluation in HE that could ensure the fulfillment of supervisors' duties. Therefore, even though students are the major consumer of higher education business activities, their interests have not received adequate consideration from education providers, which is the major reason for their withdrawal.

Likewise, the scholarly literature demonstrates that students complain in vain about their supervisors' unpleasant pedagogy practices. Some have expressed dissatisfaction in many ways, including changing supervisors and institutions. Above all the challenges, the relationship in supervision interactions has become the first aspect for students to criticize the supervision system. Indeed, most institutions have done little to deal with the students' complaints, and sadly students have no organ to advocate for and protect their learning interests. For instance, if students are not satisfied with the services they pay for (tuition fees), they do not have one to listen and ensure better service; hence they are the ones to suffer, not the institutions. As a result, higher education student attrition is increasing, where almost fifty percent of students withdraw before graduation. The ongoing scholars' debate about student attrition indicates that most difficulties come from ineffective supervision.

Indeed, the preliminary proposal in this book is to introduce the idea of establishing a supervision inspection department in each tertiary institution. The department would have different sections for monitoring and evaluating research students' supervision processes and outcomes. The officials in the unit could also support supervisors, students, and other higher education stakeholders with expert advice for functional supervision. The professionals should also deal with all supervision cases related to supervisors' qualifications and students' expectations, including their dissatisfactions and complaints.

Structurally, the supervision inspection unit in each university could have four significant divisions with different assignments related to the supervision of research students. For example, the proposed sections in this book include a supervision appointment division, where students will be assigned supervisors based on their project and discipline. Another section is assessment and training, which deals with assessing the supervision process and supporting supervisors with expert advice. Finally, the division could consist of the dispute resolution section dealing with dissatisfactions and other shortfalls in supervision objectively and the grading and certifying sub-unit. Therefore, the book discusses the duties officials in these sections would perform to support supervisors and students in succeeding in their collaboration.

However, to comprehend the author's intention and the idea of an inspection unit, she reminds readers of the school inspection at lower education levels and its revolution. Unfortunately, school inspection in most societies was a fault detection organ, but in recent years it has changed to supervision, where teachers obtain expert support in their daily teaching duties. So, the discussion in this book indicates the significance of having experts in tertiary education to support teachers and monitor their work for quality learning. Indeed, supervisors are not all-knowing or "loads," especially in this multicultural and interdisciplinary HE learning environment era; they need guidance.

Importantly, supervisors need assistance comprehending students' needs and expectations and ensuring they meet the requirement smoothly.

Historically, teachers perform well when receiving expert advice because dealing with and eradicating ignorance has been difficult. However, even if teachers are knowledgeable in their specialization area, they are not necessarily cultural and behavioral experts for all students.

So, this book consists of eight complete written chapters with different ideas that reflect the roles of teachers and the benefits of comprehending students' needs and fulfilling teaching duties. The ninth chapter is for readers to write their experiences with teachers in higher education that they think could be avoided if the institutions had a supervision inspection unit. Indeed, supervisors in higher education are teachers, and their work should be examined, evaluated, and appreciated where deserved.

The writing has twelve figures summarizing the information readers should remember. Some people learn more effectively with visual aids, so the symbols and charts can help them grasp vital ideas they do not see in the text. Some figures are the summary, and others are the main ideas for taking away.

The first chapter discusses school and teachers' inspections while describing the history of school inspections and their functionalities. The second chapter considers the evolution from school inspection to supervision and informs the school self-evaluation system. The leading cause for the change is the demand for improvement and increased knowledge of inspectors, including their roles and responsibilities. Thus, instead of reporting schools and teachers' faults to the Secretary Ministry of Education without expert support, the inspectors were required to qualify for expert roles. Therefore, they increased their understanding of the teaching profession and school development and became experts in supporting teachers and other school stakeholders.

In addition, chapter three reminds readers of the roles of committed, devoted, and passionate teachers. Teachers' commitment to learners is recognized by their ability to comprehend learners' needs and expectations. Moreover, competent teachers can collaborate with learners to strategize their learning and fulfill their learning objectives successfully. Indeed, committed, devoted, and passionate teachers are sometimes life-givers, primarily due to their ability to effectively support learners in attaining their goals. However, it might be biased to generalize teachers' perspectives as life-givers because many factors determine roles and responsibilities. For example, issues of resources, teachers' teaching skills, contextual roles, and responsibilities of teachers and learners may differ from one society to another. Therefore, the book discusses some aspects that influence the roles of teachers and peoples' diverging perceptions of teachers' responsibilities.

I also informed the current higher education structure and practices that have become complicated and that students and teachers from different backgrounds attempt to cooperate blindly. Thus, the diversity of teachers and students has brought productive and ineffective supervision experiences. In addition, some students have had challenges working with their teachers due to, among others, their perceptions of teachers' roles and responsibilities that may differ from the learning context. Contrarily, other students have collaborated with teachers and created shared learning goals and strategies to attain them.

Ultimately, the two groups may comprehend the role and responsibilities of teachers differently based on experiences and perceptions. So, students' experiences with teachers can also facilitate or hinder them from adjusting to the contextual definition of good teachers and students. However, if there was an organ dealing with supporting students and supervisors to comprehend the supervision process by explaining their roles and responsibilities in supervision, it could solve several challenges.

So, I emphasize that students must examine some aspects that define and influence the roles of teachers contextually and learn to cooperate. Thus, I discuss factors influencing teachers' roles, such as resources available and accessible in the learning institution and community. In most cases, the more students access learning resources, including information, the more independent they become, reducing the supervisors' tasks. However, teachers have more responsibilities to support learners with the required knowledge in institutions with limited resources and information. Other factors affecting supervision relate to the partners' relationships and priorities. Nevertheless, the book discusses different responsibilities higher education teachers undertake apart from supervision that may hinder them from fulfilling each student's needs and anticipations.

Unfortunately, supervisors have complete autonomy in teaching, guiding, and evaluating the students' supervision process, progress, and outcomes. Moreover, no external officials oversee their practices or appropriately correct, guide, and rebuke supervisors when they do not perform or bridge supervision ethics. Although institutions' leaders attempt to be responsible for such monitoring, most teachers remain unwavering due to their collegiate state with leaders. Consequently, students' complaints about their supervisors' practices do not obtain adequate attention or fair judgment. Instead, students are encouraged to change supervisors or drop their studies, causing emotional and financial loss when they fail to comply with supervision services.

Subsequently, supervisors' autonomy has raised several questions and kept them unanswered. First, why is there no inspection to evaluate supervisors' practices in higher education? Second, how can higher education stakeholders be confident with supervisors if student attrition increases, and most cases are associated with failure in supervision? Third, what measures must higher education stakeholders take to reduce or eliminate the student attrition challenge?

Thus, the discussion in this book may provide information for question three by proposing an establishment of a supervision department unit in each university. The department should employ experienced supervisors who are experts in student supervision, and the institution's management will not influence their work. Instead, the experts in the proposed supervision unit will collaborate to ensure adequate professional guidance in fulfilling students' learning objectives.

The book is vital for all higher education stakeholders who desire to stop or reduce student attrition caused by supervision. Keeping silent while students withdraw from their studies each semester due to incompetent supervisors is a crime. Although other factors lead to student attrition, let us cooperate and eliminate the causes associated with negligence in supervision. Indeed, parents, organizations, and societies send their loved ones to tertiary education for research degrees to acquire specific knowledge and skills. Unfortunately, half of them withdraw before graduation, and some do not attain their goal or obtain the expected knowledge and skills. The dropout tendency has caused loss to individuals, organizations, and societies that depend on universities for skilled laborers. It is time to support students to air their voices, demanding a special department to monitor and evaluate supervisors' practices.

Exceedingly, I am happy that you choose this book to join the movement demanding the establishment of a supervision inspection department where experts can oversee the work of supervisors over students and advise accordingly.

Background Information

It is unsurprising to find supervisors with long teaching experiences struggling in supervising research students today. The main reason is the change in structure and practices of higher education, where the increased number and diversity of research students is typical. Postsecondary education has changed from elite[1] learning to massification.[2] Indeed, higher education is available and accessible to all, capable academically, socially, and financially. As a tendency, most higher education institutions have established degree programs for different disciplines that traditionally could not award a degree. Besides, universities and colleges accommodate academics (especially in the Western world) from diverse backgrounds, often with varying perspectives of learning from their students.

Unfortunately, different complex issues have existed in higher education. For example, the increased number of degree programs, the huge number of students, and the diversity of student and teacher populations have created different challenges. As a result, the participants in tertiary education have diverging needs, demands, and understanding of their roles and responsibilities. Likewise, teachers must supervise many students with different backgrounds within a limited time. In addition, most partners (teachers and students) have different perceptions of their roles and how effective teaching and learning should occur. Equally, most institutions have no adequate time to guide the partners on essential and contextual learning issues or monitor their cooperation. Instead, they provide students and supervisors with a supervision handbook to read and practice the information. At the same time, the institution's leadership and management expect the partners to cooperate effectively in supervision and meet the institution and government's requirements.

Indeed, as mentioned, diversity is not only for students but supervisors. The situation demands more knowledge and understanding to cooperate and learn from each other. For example, some students' perceptions of teachers' roles may differ from their supervisors because their definitions are grounded in their cultural backgrounds and experiences regardless of contextual perceptions. Manathunga (2010, 2013, 2017) has written about the effects and challenges of a multicultural learning environment on students' and supervisors' cooperation. Reading her publications can increase the understanding of how cultural factors influences research students' learning and supervision.

Moreover, I have also written the change in structure and higher education practice in my other books (Urassa, 2020, 2021, 2022). Therefore, if you are unfamiliar with the changes I am talking about in this book, you may consult the mentioned literature and search for more knowledge that will help you comprehend the proposal in this book. For example, you may try the book "The cultural qualities you must acquire to succeed in higher education" to learn more about the current higher education learning culture and how to adapt. Another book that can support you in understanding the demand for the inspection unit for supervision is "The skills required of students to effectively collaborate with academic supervisors." The book describes challenges one may encounter based on culture and the strategies to overcome them smoothly. Therefore, cultural backgrounds influence the definitions of a good teacher and a student, which play a significant role in supervision.

Correspondingly, to demonstrate the influence of culture on learning, in their investigation of doctoral supervision, Winchester-Seeto, Homewood, Thogersen, Jacenyik-Trawoger, Manathunga, Reid, & Holbrook (2014), and Manathunga (2010, 2013) explained that mastering multicultural learning environments in higher education as a key of success. They indicated that failure to recognize the importance of cultural issues is among the challenges supervision partners encounter in their cooperation. The scholarly information explains that culture is the foundation of one's understanding and integrity and the point of reference for reasoning and practices. So, without a doubt, the supervision partners must communicate their perceptions on diverse cultural issues before constructing shared perceptions and expectations. For more information about the influence of culture in supervision and beyond, one can read the literature mentioned and others. The more one increases cultural knowledge and comprehends different higher education cultural practices, the more natural it becomes to adjust to different environments.

Therefore, according to scholarly literature, cultural change in HE is facilitated by the noticeable movement of students and academics worldwide. For instance, most postsecondary institutions in Western and Northern universities experience more students and teachers from the South and East. The academics and research students migration has never existed in such a fashion before (Marginson & van der Wende (2009), Van Der Wende (2007, 2015)). In addition, students from peripheral regions in many countries have grown to move to central and famous universities. So, students and academics from peripheral and rural areas tended to have different cultures than those from cities and developed regions that may conflict. Indeed, the movement to so-called green pastures applies to academics and students with differences other than cultures, such as gender, age, and ethnicity. Besides, these people often have different academic and social abilities that can facilitate or hinder their collaboration.

Fortunately, we now understand that the higher education learning environment is multicultural, with actors of diverse backgrounds, understanding, and practices. The movement of students and academics has developed its roots due to higher education internationalization that calls for international cooperation. The cooperation is not evenly because although Eastern and Southern origin students and scholars have moved to Northern and Western universities, there are fewer students and academics from North and West to East and South universities. The tendency of movement indicates what I call "green pasture"; people tend to move where they think will benefit, even those who claim to be volunteers; the majority volunteer where they are comfortable. They look for green pastures that are not necessarily financial but social, environmental, and even climatical.

For instance, when some students from the north and west undertake semester courses or exchange tutorial programs, they travel to enjoy the sunny weather. But, on the other hand, they do not usually travel to the East or South when they do not have anything to benefit from. Then, of course, they spend a few months of beautiful experience, and most return to their countries writing probably a stereotype report. Please do not quote me wrong here; one can live and work anywhere he feels comfortable and resourceful; the benefits can also be social, where one interacts with people and feels important. But, as a result, such inequality in the human movement has caused the accumulation of graduates in the Western and Northern societies causing a brain drain in the South and East (Marginson & van der Wende (2009), Papatsiba (2006), Van der Wende (2007, 2015)).

Similarly, the higher education actors' movement imbalance has also caused uneven multicultural learning environments. Undeniably, most universities in the western and northern are overwhelmed by the diversity of ideas and people, which can bring challenges if not well integrated. However, we understand that various and contradictory perceptions are the foundation of human development in many societies. Unfortunately, the ideas that could benefit southern and eastern people have transferred to northern and western.

Indeed, the challenges in supervision increase when students from all backgrounds fail to communicate their needs, challenges, and expectations. Some are confused due to the paradigm shift in their perceptions about teachers' responsibilities and roles in learning. Others are unfamiliar with the procedures to observe in a new learning environment when informing their anticipations. In addition, students sometimes suffer due to a lack of guidance and support in an unfamiliar learning environment. Remember, even local and indigenous students may meet with foreign supervisors and experience challenges coping. Therefore, difficulties in supervision are complex, with no respect for postsecondary participants' geographical location or supervision partners' backgrounds.

Indeed, scholarly literature demonstrates that higher education research training involves teaching and learning. The supervisors teach students to be independent researchers and acquire the skills and knowledge required. However, supervisors' practices in teaching are not monitored, supervised, or interfered with by independent institution management or inspectors. Moreover, the supervision partners do not receive expert guidance on their cooperation. Instead, as I mentioned earlier, teachers conduct, monitor, and assess the learning process, progress, and outcomes. Besides, suppose students are not satisfied with supervision practices. In that case, the typical procedure is to complain, change supervisor, or withdraw because there are no experts to deal with supervision cases to support partners in reconciliation.

Unfortunately, many supervision partnerships have broken before students' graduation due to, among others, failure to comprehend and construct shared perceptions and expectations. Likewise, some partners become frustrated, disappointed, and dissatisfied partly due to misunderstandings and diverse perceptions of roles and responsibilities.

Another issue leading to failure in supervision is resources. Indeed, we cannot deny that a lack of resources may cause supervision failure leading to students' withdrawal. For example, students who cannot access the supervisors, facilities, and other help they need might struggle to continue learning. In some cases, students have no other personnel except their supervisors, and such students tend to depend on teachers, who sometimes cannot satisfy all their needs. When the supervisors fail to fulfill students' needs, students tend to demonstrate their dissatisfaction through complaints. The process may delay their studies or cause them to drop out if they do not receive support to solve the challenges.

Therefore, several disputes may occur in the supervision process that may be difficult for partners and the institution management to resolve due to their affiliation. Undoubtedly, it is challenging for supervisors' colleagues or leaders to deal with disputes in supervision. Indeed, some students have experienced bias from the heads of departments when communicating the challenges they encounter in learning. Likewise, some leaders of the departments, institutions, and other officials discourage students from reporting their challenges, and those who inform do not receive adequate support.

Similarly, scholarly literature indicates that higher education supervision is a teaching practice. Supervisors' primary task is to teach students to research and comprehend the field protocols and objectives. They also expected to lead students to comprehend the challenges they may face in seeing the gap they should fill through their project. Therefore, if the supervision is teaching, do supervisors need inspectors or supervisors to oversee their practices and advise appropriately? How is the education of research students monitored to ensure the quality of research students' supervision? Is the students' performance adequate to inform supervisors' work quality and report their practice?

In this book, we will re-examine the formal education system and monitoring of teachers' work. It will discuss the primary and secondary teachers' tasks and school heads' involvement in the inspection. The book describes the transformation from assessment to supervision in primary and secondary schools. Teachers' tasks at these levels (primary and secondary schools) are scrutinized, questioned, and monitored in many countries and obtain expert support. Likewise, the book informs the history of the school inspection system, which started in the 1800s in many countries.

In the beginning, inspectors were not a helping hand for teachers in most cases, but the reformation occurred, where they acquired knowledge to qualify them as experts. The inspectors' main task is to monitor the teaching and learning process and assess school resource availability and accessibilities. Thus, they observe students' classroom understanding and teacher interaction while providing expert guidance. They also inform the school's well-being of the policymakers to formulate appropriate policies that can enhance student learning.

Contrary to primary and secondary levels of education, supervision in higher education, for some reason, is abandoned in the hands of supervisors without monitoring or inspection. At the same time, we read from the literature about the challenges supervisors and students encounter in supervision and hopelessness situation students face. Likewise, as mentioned earlier, higher education student attrition increases in most universities regardless of the degree structure (online and physical settings) and practices. For instance, students studying online and in a physical setting experience supervision challenges that lead to delay and dropout. Regrettably, many cases that lead to student attrition could be solved. Still, they do not reach the relevant desk for resolution partly because most institutions lack experts with adequate time and knowledge to deal with such cases fairly.

Therefore, establishing an independent supervision unit for research students could benefit all higher education stakeholders. The team could consist of experienced professors and educators who can provide their expertise in supervision and resolve disputes between the partners. They could also ensure that partners comprehend their contextual roles and responsibilities. Their understanding could support them in cooperating within the required rules and regulations while meeting their learning objectives. In such a manner, students could receive the best service from their supervisors to complete their studies and fulfill their needs and expectations.

In this book, I design a figure indicating aspects vital for establishing a supervision unit for research students. The absence of independent organs for supervision is among the changes postsecondary institutions require to improve student supervision. I believe the explanation in this background section brings an understanding to your mind that can help support the motion. As shown in Figure one, the challenges in higher education supervision are in a vicious cycle without an outlet. Therefore, monitoring and evaluating the supervision process and especially teachers' practices may be a sustainable solution for student attrition caused by weaknesses in supervision.

Figure 1. Supervision Challenges in Virtual Circle

Students and academic diversities have caused significant challenges in research student supervision. First, there is uncertainty about the qualities of supervisors academically and socially. Second, changes in structure and practices in the postsecondary education system have created a complex learning environment in a multicultural and interdisciplinary fashion. Third, the mixed environment has actors with different perceptions of the roles and responsibilities (duties) of teachers and students, which may cause challenges in supervision. Besides, research students have challenges accessing the resources they need and require for their learning. Aspects are not ranked but listed, and all affect supervision in one way or the other.

Unfortunately, students have no one to advocate for them when they complain because their teachers are the ones who control, evaluate, and monitor the supervision process, progress, and outcomes. In most cases, the complaints end at the hands of supervisors' colleagues who fail to be objective. Therefore, universities must establish independent supervision units with different sections and officials who objectively deal with supervision cases.

Chapter I

1.1 School and Teachers' Inspection

School inspection is not a new phenomenon, but old with strong and meaningful history. The primary aim of the first established school inspection was to monitor teachers' qualifications and practices. After that, the inspectors' tasks expanded to perform general and complete school inspections beyond teaching issues. Indeed, school inspection today includes several aspects, but mainly checking teachers' credentials in teaching and interaction with students and other school stakeholders.

Therefore, the work of inspectors is mainly to support teachers' employers (the Secretary Ministry of Education/or private) in comprehending teachers' qualifications and inform whether they fulfilled employers' demands. In addition, it is a measure to examine whether teachers are loyal to observing the learning curriculum, syllabus, and teaching code of conduct. Furthermore, the inspection discloses the strengths and weaknesses of schools' learning resources, including teaching and learning aids, and whether resources are accessible to teachers and learners.

Although I will describe school inspection in this chapter, I am not providing details of the specific inspectors' duties but general procedures because sometimes their duties are contextual and differ from one school to another, region to another, and country to another. Therefore, one should search for literature concerning the school or area of interest to comprehend a contextual school inspection practice. However, some people may desire a historical background of school inspection and its general functionalities. Therefore, I include the information to refresh the mind of those who have forgotten or are unfamiliar with the origin of school assessment, monitoring, and evaluation through inspection.

1.2 The History of School Inspection

School inspection has a long history that most experienced teachers can relate to. They may remember the stress, panic, and preparation they performed when receiving inspectors' visitation information. According to Marzano, Frontier & Livingston (2011), the school inspection began monitoring and assessing primary school teaching and learning processes. The term and the process originated in British and American schools, followed by other European countries. For example, in France, De Grauwe (2007) reported that the first inspection happened during Napoleon's regime at the end of the 18th century. According to Lawton & Gordon (1987) and Lillis (1992), in Britain, inspection in primary schools commenced in 1839 to monitor public funds. Other sources inform that it was an idea from Her Majesty Queen Victoria, who desired to receive a report about public money provided to schools then. Indeed, two school inspectors were appointed and acquired Her Majesty's Inspectors of School identity. They were responsible for informing the Queen about the money and ensuring the meeting of its intended purposes.

Later, the need to assess, measure, and monitor the school learning activities were substantial. So, in the same century, inspectors' numbers increased to cater to the need to inspect schools regularly, focusing on teachers' qualifications and performances in facilitating students' learning. The formulation of the education act 1992 in England and Wales explains the tasks of school inspectors in detail. Therefore, inspectors practice checkups in primary and secondary schools in England and Wales separately through two departments, thus, The Office for the Standards in Education in England and Her Majesty's Chief Inspector in Wales (Thomas 1998). The idea of school inspection spread alongside colonialism in commonwealth countries, where they practice the British education system.

Furthermore, Marzano, Frontier & Livingston (2011) informed that the criterion in assessing learning varied and sometimes created enormous and unnecessary power over teachers' activities. It also led to anxiety among heads of schools and managers because the inspectors tended to find and report faults without providing expert support. The full inspection of schools focused on assessing and monitoring learning, the resources, teachers' competencies, and the quality of instruction. The teaching quality was measured by observing how teachers mastered the learning contents, engaged students in learning, and applied appropriate teaching aids. However, the school inspection was mainly visitation, and the monitoring was associated with hierarchical and bureaucratic governing methods. Thus, although inspectors applied a few hours to assess the classrooms' learning situation, their assessment was vital and highly considered.

The school inspectors could get into a classroom, observe teachers in one or more teaching sessions, and evaluate their teaching capability accordingly. Often, a teacher could be assessed by what happened within the inspection session regardless of how he performed on other days. The short assessment hours (most of the time, 45 to 90 minutes) were adequate for the inspectors to decide on the learning and the teacher's qualities. It affected the assessment if the teacher had a terrible day and did not cooperate effectively with learners on the inspection minutes. The evaluation was one of the significant criteria that supported the governments in understanding their teachers' quality for employment, promotion, and termination purposes.

There were essential qualities in teachers that the inspectors were interested in observing. Besides, they evaluated the learning contents, the teaching methods, learning and teaching aids, their application in the lesson, and students' involvement in sessions. Furthermore, they examined whether the contents were relevant to students' understanding and requirements and whether teachers respected the syllabus and curriculum. Further, the inspectors scrutinized the lesson plans to investigate the teachers' ability to harmonize the learning contents and methods and whether they taught what they intended. In addition, the lesson plan indicated the students' and the teachers' activities and the time utilization. Therefore, the well pre-preparation of lessons informed how competent the teachers were, and vice versa was also the case.

A well-prepared lesson plan consists of the topic and content in the discussion, the teaching methods to apply, and the teaching materials to support learners. The materials could be specimens, textbooks, chemicals (for science experiments), or other items the teacher intended to engage the students. Another information lesson plan provided was the teacher and the students' tasks in the learning session. The division of duties between teachers and students was vital and the central area of interest to most inspectors. Besides, it demonstrated an understanding of the importance and strategies to engage students in the lesson.

Moreover, the plan indicated learning steps and the time for each learning stage. Teachers typically prepared four major learning stages in each lesson; the first phase that most teachers observed was the introduction, where they introduced a learning session. The overview was conducted by reminding students of the previous lesson (if applicable, the teacher could determine what students understood about the topic) through questions. The responses to the questions could provide feedback on whether students were ready for the lesson or if the teacher had to reframe the plan or adjust to the learners' needs and understanding.

Sometimes, the teacher could repeat the previously learned materials or collaborate with students to determine the appropriate contents based on the previous teaching and the syllabus. For example, if the lesson were for, let us say, forty-five minutes, a teacher could use five minutes to introduce (as part of the evaluation) the lesson and start the new task or repeat the previous one based on the response from the students. The teacher could observe whether students were ready for the newly planned lesson materials through the introduction. If they were uncertain about the previous material that could support them in understanding the scheduled lesson, the teacher had to repeat the earlier study to ensure students could learn the new material. Thus, teaching the newly prepared content for a lesson of forty-five minutes could take almost twenty-five minutes or half an hour by interacting with and including students through dialogue and questions. Learning duration mainly depended on whether the lesson was single or double, meaning forty-five or ninety minutes. The ninety minutes could accommodate a short forty-five-minute break for students and teachers to stretch and refresh.

To make my explanation understandable, let me focus on forty-five minutes lesson plan. So, after teaching the new lesson, the teacher could provide an assignment that students had to solve in the classroom for almost ten minutes. Then, when the students were busy with their studies, the teacher could check their work and provide individual feedback. In the old days, group work was not the standard of learning; instead, individual assignments dominated most learning arenas in most countries. Therefore, after the students completed their planned studies, the teacher could utilize the rest of the five minutes to summarize and emphasize the main points that he desired students to remember or work on further; sometimes, the summary could be part of the assignments.

Most of the time, teaching the new lessons was practical for school inspectors to examine and assess the quality. The focus was on student involvement, content reliability, and validity while analyzing the ability of teachers to lead students and utilize time effectively. They were also interested in the feedback and evaluation students, and teachers performed. In most cases, a qualified teacher had to involve students in learning and participate actively by performing practical activities, including asking questions. Sometimes, the teacher had to include students by asking them to complete the intended learning tasks, asking them questions, or combining different strategies depending on the learning content and objectives.

However, teachers were not obliged to provide answers to every question from students. Sometimes, a teacher could refuse tactically to respond to questions and ask the students to find answers themselves. Often, teachers' qualities were not measured by how they presented answers to students' questions but by students' involvement in finding solutions to their inquiries. Therefore, teachers could indicate the literature supporting students to obtain the answers without resolving their issues. However, some teachers could widely respond to students' problems without asking them to find knowledge elsewhere (spoon-feeding), depending on the resources. For instance, if the students have no access to necessary learning materials that may support them in answering their questions, the teacher could be the students' savior. In most cases, three main factors affect teachers' teaching style, thus, learners' ability, the subject, and resources, including the time frame.

Thus, most school inspectors were against teachers' spoon-feeding behavior and desired to observe students' involvement. Therefore, they preferred seeing students engaged actively in learning and finding solutions for the questions they asked and assignments. However, it depended on the resources students accessed to solve the learning challenges; the more resources the institutions had and were accessible to students, the more they minimized the teachers' tasks and spoon-feeding habits. Therefore, the lesson plan had to indicate the strategies to engage, motivate, and assess students' understanding.

Some lesson plans could indicate more than what I mentioned in this section, but the stated procedures of a lesson plan are the essential areas most school inspectors observed. Although I describe what happened in the past with school/teachers' inspections, the same procedures apply today in some parts of the globe. Undoubtedly, several changes have occurred in assessing and monitoring the work of teachers, but the aim remains, thus, to improve the quality of learners' learning process and outcomes.

Let us examine a lesson plan for forty-five minutes.

An Example of a Forty-five Minute Lesson Plan

A lesson plan typically has three sections. The teacher writes the lesson's objectives and learning materials in the first section.

The lesson plan shows three significant sections, the introduction, the lesson procedure, and the conclusion.

The first part

The lesson plan for standard----------------------the topic of -----------

Year/Date..

The main objective...

The specific objectives...

The number of students..

Second Part

Time/ minutes	Teacher's activities	Learners' activities	Teaching and learning materials	Comments about activities
1-5 min	Introduce the lesson. How, by asking questions on the previous lesson. And mentioning the headlines of the new session	Respond to the questions and ask if any. Note the headings.	It depends on the nature of the topic	The teacher should indicate whether the lesson was successful or not, with explanations
1-25 min	Discussing the lesson intended How, by involving the students in the discussion through questions	Listening and responding to the activities provided to them. Ask questions. if any	Computer, publications, or any other object or subject	
1-10 min	Providing students with assignments to measure their understanding	Responding to the assignment and asking questions, if any	It depends on the nature of the topic and assignment	
1-5 min	Summarize the learned lesson and maybe provide students with homework, further readings, or recommendations	Listening and asking for clarification where needed Understand and note the instruction	It depends on the nature of the topic and the instruction provided	
General assessment	To assess the effectiveness of the learning session; the strategies and support provided to students	To assess students' engagement	Assess the efficiency of the materials	

The Third Part of the Lesson Plan

Conclusion

Comments from the teacher (the level of success)

The signatures

Teacher's signature (the instructor)

Class leader's signature (a responsible student representative)

Usually, the lesson plan consists of five main aspects: the duration of the lesson, the teacher's task, the students' activities, contents/learning materials, and the comments/assessment concerning the attainment of the lesson's objectives. The time allocated for the learning session must suffice the scope of the content and activities for the teacher and students. The teacher evaluated each learning stage (introduction, the leading discussion, and the conclusion) and the recommendation he provided. If the intended lesson was unsuccessful, the teacher should indicate the reason and measures to rectify the deficit. One of the measures could be to repeat the class by applying a different approach that could change students' activities, materials, and the like. Alternatively, they could invite an expert on the topic for more clarification or visit the physical setting that can explain the situation better, and so on.

After the teachers' assessment, the school inspectors received the lesson plan to examine the teacher's suggestion and analyze his satisfaction with his teaching. Teachers' evaluations of the lesson were vital and typically a point of discussion compared with the inspector's point of view to find a shared consensus. The clear lesson plans were helpful for the teacher in charge and others assigned to teach the same class afterward. The information could be apparent to others what the students had learned in the contents and their level of understanding. Such information was vital to help a new teacher decide to continue or repeat the previously learned material or topic.

Therefore, the school inspector used to assess the lesson plan and observe actual teaching in a classroom. They evaluated how teachers included their learners in learning and their relationships (teachers/students' interactions). Examining the contents' correctness based on the curriculum and syllabus was among the inspectors' concerns. The curriculum was vital due to the centralization of examinations and education in most regions in the old days. The syllabus was another document they scrutinized to evaluate the quality of the contents and adherence.

Moreover, the school inspectors examined the feedback provided to the learners and its effects on their learning (motivating or discouraging). Indeed, some teachers are competent in delivering motivational feedback, and others do the opposite. Therefore, the assessment of feedback teachers presented to students verbally and in writing was among the aspects inspectors were interested in observing. However, the inspectors noted that some teachers could not motivate students with their feedback during the inspection. Unfortunately, sometimes inspectors reported the weakness without supporting teachers with appropriate advice, partly because they lacked knowledge and skills in teaching the specific subjects.

In addition, school inspectors examined the documents associated with students' attendance and performance in different subjects. They dealt with formative test scores and feedback, including the follow-ups in such activities. The investigation was vital to inform inspectors of the progress and connection between the previous and present lessons. It also declares the students' understanding of the content and readiness for the summative examinations. Furthermore, it could support inspectors in predicting the progress and the outcomes expected of teachers and students in their learning. Whenever the results were less than expected, where the students failed to comprehend the learning contents, it demonstrated teachers' weaknesses. Thus, teachers' weak points were among the issues reported to the Secretary Ministry of Education or any other organ responsible for teachers' employment at that time.

Furthermore, the inspectors had to interview teachers, students, school leaders, and other relevant school stakeholders. These were people who could inform the school's academic, financial, and social state, including the availability of resources, workforce, and learning materials. The inspectors desired to learn almost everything in schools, and the more information they gathered, the more they understood the learning and teaching challenges and teachers' qualities.

The school inspectors received information from the other stakeholders about the schools' well-being in physical learning environments, including buildings, teaching facilities, and security. According to Brimblecombe, Ormston & Shaw (1995), the old days' inspection was stressful for many heads of schools and teachers due to its fault-finding nature. However, another main criterion that determined the evaluation of teachers apart from the mentioned learners' ability, resources, and subject (science, arts) was the nature of the school (boarding, day, boys, girls, or co-education). Thus, these criteria supported inspectors in choosing the main aspects to investigate apart from the general. For example, inspectors examined students' living conditions in boarding schools, including accommodation and food quality.

As shown in Figure two, one can summarize the aspects and qualities of teachers the inspectors were interested in examining.

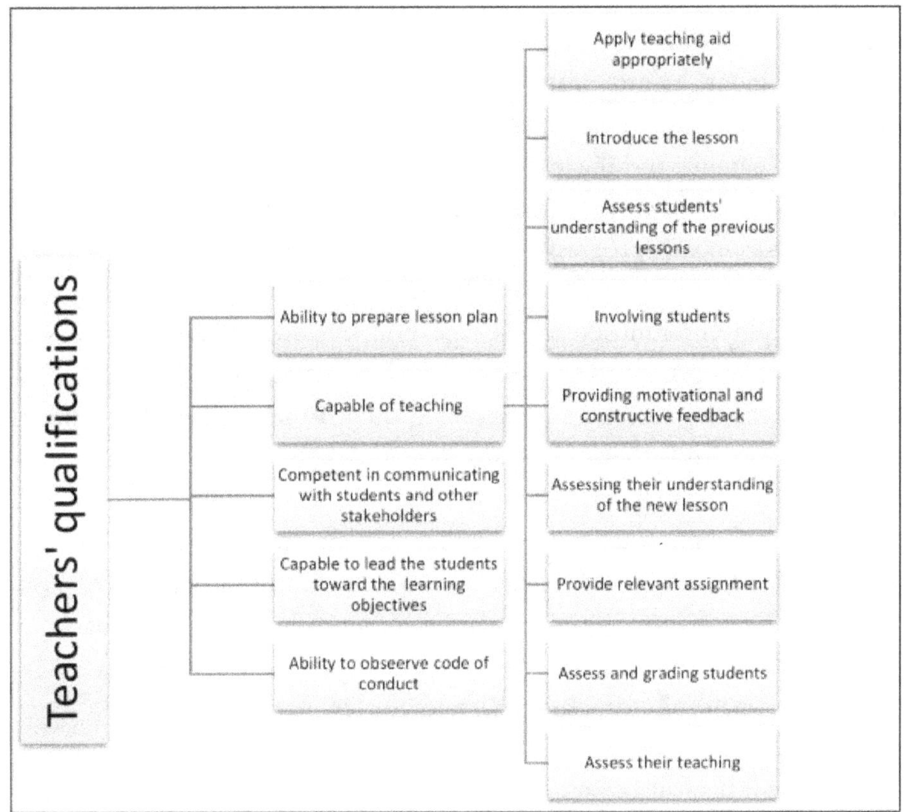

Figure 2. Teachers' Qualifications that Inspectors Observed

Figure two indicates that teachers' qualifications that inspectors were interested in scrutinizing were many, but importantly, teachers had to be able to prepare a lesson for the students. Moreover, he had to communicate with students and other stakeholders appropriately and professionally. At the same time, teachers were leaders to head students toward fulfilling learning objectives while observing the code of conduct. Therefore, the essential qualification was teaching ability, where teachers had to demonstrate their ability to apply teaching aid, introducing lessons to students while assessing students' understanding of the previous lessons.

Moreover, the teachers' ability to involve learners in learning while providing constructive and motivational feedback was vital for the inspectors to observe.

Indeed, good teachers display their ability to assess students' understanding, provide relevant assignments, and grade students accordingly. Finally, as mentioned earlier, all teachers had to evaluate their teaching and record their evaluation in part three of the lesson plan.

In most regions, school inspectors could obtain information concerning challenges between students and teachers and those between teachers with themselves, parents, and the leadership. Thus, they touched on almost all areas of learning and teachers' tasks and relations, thus the leadership and students' learning process and progress). School inspectors reported their evaluation and provided recommendations to the Secretary Ministry of Education (the primary employer for most teachers in government-owned institutions in many countries) or any other appropriate organ which requested the inspection.

Unfortunately, inspectors were appointed due to their knowledge about the school system and their reputation in the community, not necessarily experience in teaching. Therefore, the appointment of inspectors and their practices challenge teachers and other school stakeholders in receiving professional advice. However, one can comment that most people who joined the teaching profession in the old days were more committed and passionate about helping learners attain their learning goals. Besides, education was provided as one of the vital social services for few to prepare them for specific assignments rather than profitable business projects.

The argument that the old system was better than the current may demonstrate bias due to the information Connell and Manathunga (2012) provided concerning the weaknesses in the supervision of doctoral degrees in the old days. Likewise, the statement may mislead where some may think I disregard the effort and commitment most teachers express today to their learners' success. So, comparing the old and current teachers' responsibilities should be a topic of interest for another time or book. However, regular school inspections, whether in the lower levels of education or tertiary, undoubtedly reinforced teachers' commitment to the learners' success. They know someone checks on them and appreciates their work and, by so doing, increases learning qualities. Indeed, the school inspection was complex, with diverse duties for inspectors, as summarized in Figure three.

Figure 3. The Essential School Inspectors' Duties

Figure three summarizes the school inspectors' duties in the old days. The illustration indicates that the main task of inspectors was to act as a disciplinary organ for teachers while monitoring the quality of education. In addition, they had to safeguard the government's interests and report the teachers' and schools' shortfalls. Therefore, school inspectors emphasized lesson plans as an instrument for their investigation while monitoring and evaluating the teaching and learning process in a specific learning setting.

Simultaneously, they focused on the psychosocial learning environment between the learners and their teachers. Inspectors examined the physical learning environment, such as building facilities, while finding the faults and reporting them to the relevant organ. Although some had no expertise in the subjects or teaching methods, they knew the school system and community's needs. They also demonstrated authoritative leadership to teachers, and their evaluation impacted teachers' employment, promotions, and termination.

Therefore, today's school inspection follows the procedure explained in the old day's inspection, but inspectors' duties, qualifications, and relationships with other school stakeholders have changed. In addition, the name for school quality control has changed from inspection to supervision in many regions, mainly because the current inspectors have the qualifications that benefit school stakeholders to improve their performance. Indeed, most inspectors have acquired subject expertise and the teaching methodology to support teachers in rectifying their weaknesses and improving the learning process and outcomes. Indeed, most of them have become supporting agencies for teachers and school leaders, aiming at solving problems rather than reporting the faults, hence evolution.

Chapter 2

2.1 From School Inspection to Supervision

In the previous chapter, I discussed the procedures and areas that school inspectors were interested in observing. However, we also see that inspectors' functions changed after the acquisition of expert qualifications. Different literature indicates the evolution of school monitoring and evaluation system in many countries. For example, Burke and Krey (2005) provided historical information about school inspections, describing the weaknesses of the then-school monitoring system. They primarily mentioned the inspectors' judgmental tendency that discouraged teachers and caused school uncertainty. Their nature of finding teachers and other school actors' faults without providing constructive feedback to solve problems was one of the challenges faced by school inspection.

In addition, the school inspection team consisted of people with no expertise in subjects and teaching methods but community knowledge. Likewise, the inspectors distance themselves from the school and the people they inspect by visiting schools when it suits them. Indeed, it was stressful for teachers and the heads of schools as they worried about the amount of fault the inspectors would point fingers at and had no hope of gaining support from the inspectors (Fearon1889).

Consequently, there has been continuous development in monitoring school development and assessing teachers' work. However, as we have seen, a significant change has occurred concerning inspectors' requirements, including their qualifications and duties. We may remind ourselves of the situation at the beginning of the school inspection system, which started with a specific project initiated by the majesty Queen Victoria. After that, the school inspection system became regular, even when inspectors were not professional teachers. However, the inspectors were prudent enough to report the schools' and teachers' development and issues that needed change. Unfortunately, they had unnecessary power over teachers and school heads, sometimes creating difficulties working together. In addition, although they observed teachers in a classroom, most inspectors were not educators and lacked teaching expertise (Marzano et al., 2011).

Indeed, their actions made teachers prepare their teaching and follow the rules and teaching ethics. However, the inspection became unfruitful over time due to inspectors' lack of teaching qualifications and subject knowledge that could help them provide professional advice. Sometimes, inspectors worked mechanically, following the employer's instructions without supporting teachers and other school stakeholders for improvement. As a result, according to Brimblecombe, Ormston & Shaw (1995), teachers experienced school inspection process stress, unfruitfulness, and tiresome. Indeed, teachers and other school actors had to prepare for inspection and even prepare learners for it to cover their weaknesses.

Thus, nothing is static, especially when people are awakening and experiencing a burden. So, the weaknesses in the inspection system called for change, demanding inspectors' subject know-how and teaching qualifications. As a result, some had to join teaching colleges to gain the required knowledge and skills. Others had to enroll in short courses that increased their understanding of specific subjects and teaching methods. Hence, the increase in inspectors' qualifications in subject matter and teaching methodology led to more effective cooperation with school stakeholders in the inspection. Indeed, the birth of the name supervision over the school inspection came with new perspectives of quality assurance and empowering inspectors to provide expert advice to teachers rather than reporting their faults to their employers and school owners.

Even though the name of the school inspector has not changed in some regions, the inspection procedures and inspectors' duties are not similar to the old days. Undoubtedly, the weaknesses in inspection led to the current school supervision. Some parts of the globe call the transformed school inspection "quality monitoring," but others have continued with the name "school inspection." The transformation is not merely the name but mainly in supervisors' qualifications and duties and school inspectors' knowledge of the subject they inspect and its teaching technique. Currently, the inspection process focuses on supporting school stakeholders to perceive their abilities and weaknesses, aiming to improve their performance to the standard required for student learning. Thus, the reform for inspectors' qualifications and process legitimates the primary aim of a school inspection, thus improving students' learning regardless of other factors such as resources, teaching process, teachers' qualifications, and the like.

The inspectors' qualifications have also become number one in allocating their roles and responsibilities. They have diverse specialties which determine their duties in the process, such as subject and level of education. Thus, primary schools, secondary schools, and higher education supervisors exist. The supervisors' specialization in some regions is essential in primary and secondary schools. For example, if an inspector should observe a history teacher in her teaching, he must have studied history and have acquired a history teaching methodology. Contrary, some regions insist on inspectors' mastering the general teaching approach to advise teachers regardless of their specializations. Ultimately, the school inspectors' qualifications have acted as a catalyst for the change of inspection practices leading to meaningful supervision.

A paradigm shift has also occurred in the relationship between the school actors and supervisors. While the visitation system created a distance between the school inspectors and other school stakeholders, causing difficulty in advising and problem-solving, the new system operates in some regions. For example, in the Scandinavian countries, the system has changed to self-school inspection (school self-evaluation), where supervisors (inspectors) collaborate with school leadership daily. In these countries, a school inspector is part of leadership and plans for learning in collaboration with teachers and the head of school in the learning setting. Supervisors are among the school employees; they inspect learning activities and are available and accessible whenever needed. Consequently, the system has minimized the distance visitation inspection created, and the schools' actors collaborate with the inspector to strategize learning and solve daily challenges.

In some parts of the world, according to Kemethofer, Gustafsson, & Altrichter (2017), the decentralization[3] of the school inspection system has allowed the inspectors to report their teaching and learning findings to the school heads. So, in collaboration, the leaders, and the inspectors, discuss the inspection outcomes and support or solve challenges accordingly. In most cases, the school heads cooperate with inspectors to support teachers and students in learning. They perform such a scheme by investigating the accessibility of teaching and learning resources. Further, they scrutinize teachers' availability and qualifications and students' well-being while assisting them appropriately.

In other words, self-evaluation is a system of decentralizing supervision and empowering the head of schools and inspectors. Thus, the decentralizing inspectorate practices have empowered them to collaborate in solving schools' challenges. In such a situation, the inspectors ensure that school actors (leaders, students, and teachers) cooperate appropriately and harmoniously work with each other to facilitate students learning. Therefore, the school inspection system's decentralization has been vital in some countries since the 1990s.

Indeed, formal education systems have changed, and stakeholders need to cope with changes. For instance, the change from centralization to decentralization and the demand for inspectors' teaching qualifications are among the newly introduced practices. Another change is the change of focus on inspectors' qualifications from non-educational backgrounds to educational professionals. The scholarly literature indicates that the school inspectorate has become the most effective system for evaluating learning and teaching quality. Although the decentralization system, the inspectors integrate with other school actors, and their responsibilities remain to monitor and assess the learning process.

The number of inspectors may also vary, where some schools have more than one inspector dealing with assessing the quality of teaching. The primary attribute of an inspector/supervisor is to be objective, independent, and intelligent in understanding the priorities and working with other school stakeholders. In some cases, it is like having a department with one member or two in the school dealing with the quality of learning. They are also available and responsible for providing expert advice to school heads and other actors when needed, cooperatively and individually.

2.1.1 Decentralization Era

The change from inspection to supervision was necessary partly to cater to individual school needs. The emergence of private schools in the 1990s in many countries created a challenge in monitoring the quality of learning. The development emerged due to governments' resource limits allowing private organizations to provide formal education. Indeed, the policy brought different challenges in monitoring and evaluating schools. For example, one professor informed that noticeable variations in school resources and teachers' qualifications were vivid and required a new perspective to assess their performance. He shared his experience in Sweden and asserted that "no one prepared for such change where *private organizations and people could supply education. It was like the government failed to care for her citizen allowing variation of the quality of education.*" His experience was not limited to Sweden; I have heard from diverse people about the uncertainty private schools brought in school monitoring and evaluation system worldwide. In addition, in some regions, the governments and private schools brought changes in schools' financing system, including the payment for inspectors. As a result, the schools have obtained mandatory funds to raise and allocate them based on their contextual needs.

Jonathan, one school inspector in one commonwealth country, asserted, *"The school inspection was inferior to some schools when private schools emerged. Mhh... because most private schools had resources more than the standard inspectors expected, and their teachers had more than the qualifications required in public schools. For example, some primary school teachers graduated with bachelor's degrees and others with master's degrees. While in public school, diplomas were the acceptable standard teachers' qualifications. Moreover, the students had a more conducive learning environment than most government-owned schools. So,... school inspection in such well-equipped private schools did not challenge quality; instead, inspectors realized the resources which lacked in public schools and argued the government to fulfill."*

Mr. Jonathan informed me what is more familiar to many private schools than the public. Indeed, some private schools have resources that the public does not have, and others lack the basic resources, affecting the quality of student learning and outcomes. However, the inspectors' report on variation in these two sectors (private and public) supported the policymakers in allowing the school to operate or close. In addition, the inspection findings support policymakers in permitting public schools' management to raise funds to acquire the necessary resources for students learning. It does not mean the governments are not financing their schools, but schools are encouraged to find other sources of income for their needs. Indeed, where fundraising is applicable and inspection is decentralized, the schools' heads, teachers, and inspectors should collaborate to identify scarce resources and formulate donation systems. However, inspectors' involvement in funding arrangements may affect their commitment to monitoring and evaluating schools objectively.

Conversely, in most countries where decentralization of inspection has occurred, school heads are empowered to conduct school self-evaluation in collaboration with inspectors who are part of school leadership. The school actors discussed the collected inspection information for change, adjustment, or enhancement. The aim is to deliver the standard of education expected of their learners and other school stakeholders. As a result, teachers regularly obtain constructive feedback on their work, reflect on their performance, make changes, aim high, and receive rewards accordingly.

There are many changes in school inspection structure and practices, which can be interesting to comprehend. One can read other publications from different countries and realize the diversity in monitoring and evaluating the quality of instruction in schools. Reviewing literature can widen one's knowledge about school inspection and its evolution. I recommend Ehren, Gustafsson, Altrichter, Skedsmo, Kemethofer & Huber (2015), Chapman (2001), Courtney (2016), Cusack (1992), Ehren, Gustafsson, Altrichter, Skedsmo, Kemethofer & Huber (2015), Hall (2017), MacBeath (2006) or others that can provide better and current insight on the topic.

For example, Ehren, Gustafsson, Altrichter, Skedsmo, Kemethofer & Huber (2015) and MacBeath (2006) attempted to compare some European countries' school inspections. Reading their explanation can provide a better picture of school inspection decentralization and school self-inspection. They also indicated the relationship change between inspectors and other school actors that can be interesting to learn. Likewise, Hall (2017) provided details about school inspection in Scandinavian countries, indicating changes from distance inspection to close and inseparable school commitment.

However, regardless of whether the school inspection is in the form of visitation or school self-evaluation, the aims remain to assess learning activities and ensure the availability of resources. In addition, the inspectors provide professional standpoints, strengthen cooperation between and among the schools' actors, and record updated information about the state of the schools and learning. Therefore, school inspection activities are vital for policymakers and school management in formulating policies and regulating resource provision and utilization.

Learning activities can be more effective when the cooperation between the school actors and inspectors is fruitful. For instance, in the current school supervision we just discussed, the inspectors are mainly experts in most schools and no longer faultfinders. Instead, they support teaching agencies in teaching and demonstrating the contextual techniques that enhance students' learning. The school self-evaluation system is also expanding its territory, and many European countries have adopted it. Thus, undeniably, the system has become a catalyst for the new birth of supervision expertise at primary and secondary levels of education.

As a result, school supervision has become more helpful to school actors because inspectors can share knowledge and skills with school actors and correct mistakes rather than merely report their faults. Indeed, inspectors' qualifications have changed teachers' subordination and opened a beneficial mutual relationship. Indeed, as Marzano et al. (2011) asserted, the inspection paradigm has shifted from instruction and teachers' monitoring agents to supporters and experts. I hope the system does not minimize the hierarchical practice in formal education but indicates stress reduction compared with the old-school inspection system. Besides, it has rectified some challenges school actors face and brought harmony among and between them for better student learning.

2.2 Concepts Opposing School Inspection

Although some argue that the school inspection process is financially costly (where supervisors must visit schools), it is vital for examining students' learning quality. In most cases, teachers' activities must be monitored and evaluated to investigate the assistance required by stakeholders. Besides, teachers' activities in the classroom cannot be measured only by students' performance in formative and summative evaluation. Still, the quality of their interaction with teachers informs more than what tests and examinations display. In addition, several practices in the learning process need assessment, monitoring, and regular correction to meet learners' expectations. Therefore, the expense of inspecting schools and teachers' teaching process has not exceeded the disadvantage of not examining and evaluating the learning process.

Likewise, some argue that teachers comprehend their roles and responsibilities and that inspection is unnecessary because it increases the tension. However, uncertainty and stress during inspection mostly engulf school actors, unaware of their roles and responsibilities. So, in most cases, the inspectors' actions and procedures make teachers attentive, and the good news is that the current supervision is not for fault-finding but to provide expert support. Indeed, there are many aspects teachers need to demonstrate for their development and reward; therefore, inspectors can be a helping hand. Furthermore, monitoring and evaluating the learning process and activities have been the source of changes and growth in the formal education system. It is still the primary instrument for quality control and assurance, regardless of the level of education.

Even though some schools practice self-evaluation, as discussed earlier, the findings are still helpful in school development. For example, when inspectors visit their teaching sessions, teachers turn to the code of conduct and teaching ethics. They also demand the resources that facilitate learning, reflect on their performance, and demonstrate teaching strategies that support learners to utilize and reveal their abilities. In addition, teachers manage to prepare the learning materials appropriate for a specific group of students. Finally, they also keep themselves current by engaging in current knowledge development, such as using technology in teaching, preparing a lesson plan, and choosing teaching methods and evaluation tools.

Conversely, in most countries, supervisors are more interested in supporting learners by communicating and sharing knowledge through teachers, leaders, and direct conversations with students. In addition, some have gone far as to communicate with parents, mainly where school self-evaluation applies to strengthen school and home cooperation. In most cases, where schools and communities work together, learning challenges can be solved effectively and increase students' learning. Therefore, the school inspection practice has allowed better collaboration of school stakeholders, which is necessary.

However, the opposers of school inspection may be unaware of the evolution of school inspection. They still remember the shortfalls and do not comprehend the current inspection's advantages. In this chapter and the previous one, I have attempted to describe the inspection system changes to bring the missing awareness.

Indeed, we have seen how inspectors performed their duties without essentially supporting school actors (students, teachers, and heads), but again I have informed the inspectors' qualifications and expertise change. The change in inspectors' qualifications is the essence of evolution, where inspectors have become supporters of teaching rather than critics, providers, or reporters. Moreover, currently, inspectors provide vital information about resources and school development that are the foundation of policymakers' decisions. So, monitoring and evaluation in schools is an essential process to maintain. Finally, I mentioned some arguments the opposers of the inspection system apply, which I also indicated in Figure four.

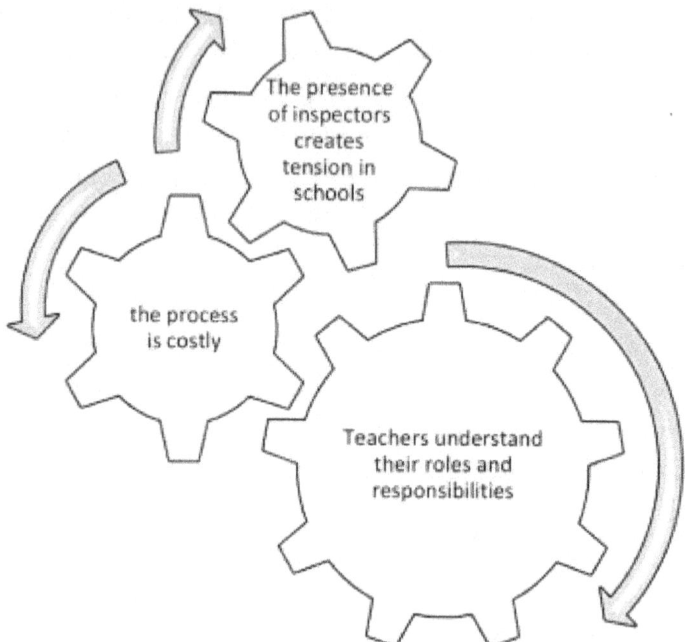

Figure 4. School Inspection Opposers' Arguments

As indicated in the figure, the opposers of school inspection have three significant views. First, the opposers argue that most teachers comprehend their roles and responsibilities, hence no need for inspection. Second, they believe the inspection process is costly and, most of the time, causes tension in schools.to inspect the process is expensive, and inspectors create tension in schools.

However, most educators understand that they need someone to oversee or discuss their work because of their roles and responsibilities' sensitivity. Teachers are the constructors of skilled laborers, and their task is vital for development. Indeed, the work of teachers is vital and needs discussion, corrections, and cooperation from different organs, including the inspection units.

Chapter 3

3.1 Teaching Profession

The teaching profession is a complex but rewarding career. People become somebody because of teachers' ability to mould them and help them discover their talents and capacity. However, teaching is a business not for everybody but for a few willing to devote their resources and provide service to others, even in a challenging environment. Honestly, it is for people eager to lift the oppressed and support them in solving their problems to acquire freedom. We must agree that nothing keeps people in captivity and oppression more than ignorance, which is teachers' primary task in meeting with learners. Many learned individuals have stories about their experiences with teachers in eliminating ignorance and building careers. So, teachers support learners to bring discoveries and be free from ignorance, sometimes beyond their expectations.

Therefore, competent teachers seek corrections, guidance, and evaluation of their work for quality assurance. I believe that teachers with a good intention of freeing their learners have no problem being corrected, guided, and evaluated because such teachers focus on the best of their learners. Moreover, overseeing teachers facilitates freeing learners from ignorance by supporting them in acquiring general and specific teaching knowledge. Most teachers are grateful for obtaining assistance, especially at the beginning of their teaching profession. We all know that eradicating a lack of knowledge is no quick-fix task; it needs time to comprehend learners' interests, needs, and expectations. Teachers should also be aware of their resources and those available and accessible in the learning institution. Besides, good relationships between teachers and learners who trust each other and formulate shared expectations are also vital. The relationship between teachers and students in learning can be functional if teachers have leadership skills. Therefore, when learners attain their objectives through formal education, it indicates teachers' good leadership, and most learners appreciate it.

Indeed, most qualified teachers understand that teaching and learning require patience, understanding, and conducive communication strategies to attain the intended learning objectives. Such teachers use time effectively to understand students' standpoints on issues or learning contents before imposing their philosophy on them. They meet learners where they are and develop their understanding of questioning their knowledge to acquire the intended learning goals. They also emphasize effective leadership that involves students in the learning process to promote their engagement for outstanding outcomes. As a result, proficient teachers can be life-givers due to their roles and responsibilities in building different and individual careers.

Contrary, today, people who join the teaching profession are not necessarily qualified. Some had no other option than to join the teaching profession, especially where joining does not demand high academic grades. In other cases, the profession does not require one's passion before selection or asking people why they want to be teachers. Yes, some institutions demand study intently, but that is not good enough to measure applicants' passion and intention in choosing the profession. Often some applicants obtain help to write the intent without thinking or understanding what that means to be a teacher.

For example, I asked one master's degree second-year student who was near to graduate the teaching profession about her intention of becoming a teacher. She admitted she did not want to join teaching, but her mother insisted. The female master's degree student had no interest in students, and according to our conversation, she was unaware of the commitment required in the profession. So, I attempted to inform her of the learners' needs and expectations, and she said that if learners demonstrated high demand, she would look for another job. Her statement made me think about how disadvantaged learners may be in a meeting with teachers with no ambition to convince them or meet their demands. But, of course, one should understand that the ignorance of learners may lead to different problems in understanding their teachers.

For this reason, teachers need to comprehend learners' understanding of the learning process, contents, and use of resources from the beginning. Having the mind to quitting the teaching job if the learners are not what the teachers expect is a lack of passion and interest in the learners' interests, needs, and expectations. A teacher who desires to meet learners who fit her descriptions and have no challenge teaching may lack passion.

So, as mentioned earlier, many reasons force people to opt for the teaching profession. Others lose their passion because they experience difficulties teaching without adequate support. Such teachers may have experienced hardship in teaching resources, school management, leadership, or other issues that have discouraged them from becoming part of the teaching community. On the other hand, they may hold on due to a lack of alternatives for their income even with such discouragement, and the situation may lead to failure to support students optimally. Figure 5 summarises the tasks of effective teachers.

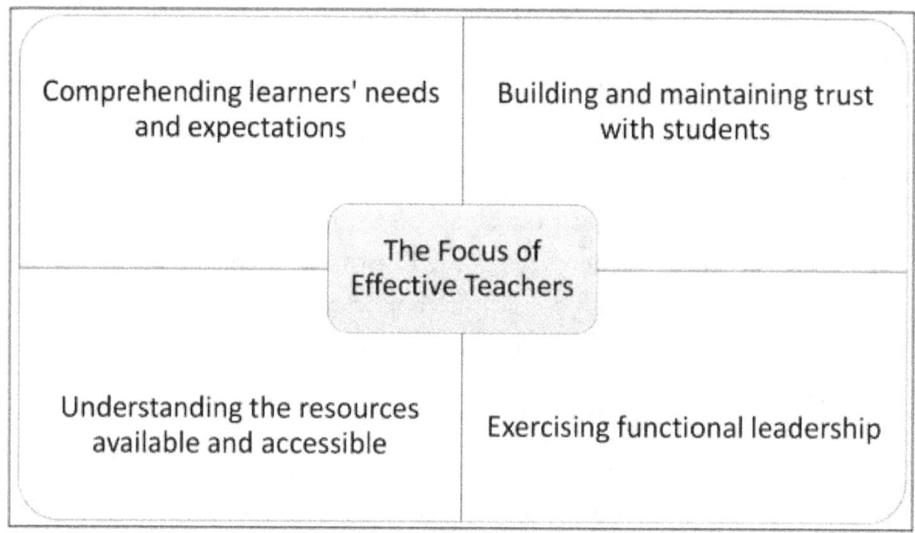

Figure 5. Four Vital Qualities of Effective Teachers

According to Figure five, a competent supervisor should understand his students' needs and expectations in learning. He must also consider building and maintaining trust for effective cooperation. Moreover, a good supervisor should consider functional leadership, which cares about students' learning ability and progress. Likewise, he must understand the resources available and accessible to students. At least, these are the basic factors that determine the quality of a supervisor.

3.1.1 Higher Education Supervisors

In the case of higher education, the situation may be different from other levels. Teachers' qualifications and employment process differ from one institution to another and from one region to another. For example, some teachers are forced to teach research students due to their knowledge of the subject matter, even when they desire to research. I use "forced" because most academics apply for a research position and automatically become research students' supervisors and teachers. On the other hand, the majority do not think they are teachers and do not even like to be called teachers. They did not apply for the teaching position, but their research performance legitimates them to qualify for higher education teaching and supervision of research students. In such a system, some may lack the passion and teaching qualifications required in the teaching profession. As a result, their weaknesses may hinder their communication and cooperation with students affecting them negatively.

However, not all universities allow researchers to teach students without special programs supporting them in acquiring teaching methodology. For example, in most Scandinavian countries and Norway, a graduate who desires to join the teaching profession usually undertakes practical pedagogical education (UIO, 2022). The programs have helped people acquire teaching methodology and not necessarily a passion for teaching. So, in most universities, the teaching profession has changed to all who have master's or doctoral degrees, not necessarily passion for students' learning.

One respectable professor from a high-ranking university, Prof. David, revealed that the teaching profession in higher education has become complex and lost its originality. He added that "*most actors need to comprehend the uniqueness of the teaching profession before engaging in it. There is a tendency for graduates with doctoral degrees to think they can join the teaching profession because of their degree, but the degree cannot make someone a good teacher... there are more qualifications needed, including the commitment to learners.*"

Indeed, higher education teachers certainly need to have more than degrees. They need inner motivation for teaching than a certificate of their performance in the field and research. The professor explained how the teaching profession functioned in the old time when his father was teaching in the early 1900s. One of the qualifications he mentioned was the commitment of teachers compared to the current era. Indeed, Professor David asserted that teachers were admirable in the old days and that teaching was among the most respectable careers.

The professor described a motto that stimulated people to think before joining the profession. Thus, "Teaching is a Call, not a Job" was the first issue the head of institutions desired to discuss with people who wanted to join the teaching profession in his community. Besides, the applicants were reminded of teachers' commitment and enthusiasm required to support learners before joining a teaching career in their community. Furthermore, the motto, "Teaching is a call, not a job," recapped teachers' dedication to teaching and serving others without focusing on personal gain. The motto is still in use today, meaning one should not join a teaching profession without passion and willingness to support learners.

Such devotion made many old-school teachers commit themselves to learners' success and were life-givers. Prof. David added that those who joined the career must comprehend that teaching needs passion and commitment to learners and society. They were also certain of the challenges associated with teaching, including compulsory overtime when correcting students' homework without extra payments. They knew learners depended on their support and had to be trustworthy role models who comprehended learners' needs and expectations. The description from Prof. David is vital and meaningful for policymakers to consider when formulating teaching policies. Indeed, everyone who desires to join the teaching profession should know the demands and the requirements. The career is rewarding for those who are passionate, comprehend learners' needs, and believe in their ability to support them. Often teachers are committed even though they have not demanded the best salary for their devotion. In addition, some qualified teachers look up to other significant non-monetary benefits in their profession, like being up-to-date in knowledge and supporting learners and societies with skilled laborers. Furthermore, teachers who perform their work effectively gain the reward of seeing their learners prosper and mentioning their names as the tools for their success. Nothing amazing as supporting people to attain their life goals and becoming part of it; yes, that is what the teaching profession does to its learners.

3.1.2 The Phenomenon "Teachers as Lifegivers"

In the old days, before the 1900s, in some societies where education was a scarce commodity, most teachers had the qualifications mentioned earlier. Indeed, teachers were life-givers to their learners, and parents trusted sending their children and loved ones to school. The concept that teachers are life-givers is associated with teachers being the primary and sometimes sole source of information and influencing learners' lives in diverse areas. In such a case, they were responsible for parenting their learners, which placed them in a higher position than the current teachers.

Therefore, one factor determining teachers' position is resource availability (material and human) in the institution and its accessibility to the students. So, the needier the institution and societies were for resources, including information, the more the teachers' importance increased, the busier they became, and the higher their ranking. They were needed more as a source of knowledge because there was nowhere else to turn for information and learning. In addition, teachers were involved in politics, religion, and policymaking activities, which increased their contribution to information and strengthened their power and position in decision-making.

Remember, the rapid social media and technological development emanated a few decades ago. Besides, communication improvement has not increased in many societies, and some current development is incomparable. So, before technology development, teachers were the primary source of information for most families, and their messages to their learners were influential. I am talking about societies with low technological development, limited resources, and desperately needing teachers. When the learners need teachers' support desperately, their values increase, and teachers may need more help from the institution's leadership and management than before.

On the contrary, the community with different situations, such as adequate resources, including diverse sources of information, may regard teachers differently. The availability of resources affects students' and teachers' roles in learning and how they cooperate and perform their duties. For instance, if the institution has adequate learning resources such as publications and supportive learning agencies apart from supervisors, the roles of teachers change from sole source of knowledge to companion to the learners. However, when students lack vital publications, they may depend on teachers to access up-to-date information, increasing teachers' responsibilities. In all cases, the more responsible teachers become, the increase their power over learners and the more dependent learners become.

Nevertheless, regardless of the availability and accessibility of resources and information technology, the roles of teachers will always vary. Likewise, learners' ability to recognize their needs and learn independently influences teachers' duties regardless of other factors. Currently, most higher education learning environments are multicultural, with different people of diverse views. For example, students' diversity and functionality in higher education are vivid and need teachers' attention to study them.

Indeed, most higher education institutions accommodate students with different abilities and diverging perspectives on teachers' roles. Some could work more independently but have different mindsets than most in the contextual learning environment. Awkwardly, some students attempt to transfer their perspectives on teachers' roles from one learning environment to another. The danger to their practice is that teachers' roles and responsibilities are based on contextual resources and other factors. As a result, they ignore their roles and responsibilities or overshadow teachers' presence altogether. Although such students comprehend the role and responsibilities of their teachers, they may fail to cooperate if their understanding is different from the contextual perspectives.

Therefore, the essential issue all research students must address before enrolling in higher education or soon after the enrolment is finding teachers' contextual roles and responsibilities. They must avoid assumptions and generalizing teachers' tasks because the resources, including information accessibility in most cases, determine teachers' roles in students' learning. So, investigating contextual theory to recognize the status and role of teachers has not been a time waste. If teachers' responsibilities differ from students' experiences or expectations, the partners must communicate to establish a shared perception of roles and responsibilities and create shared expectations.

However, in most cases, some research students in many societies still recognize teachers as life-givers, regardless of their accessibility to resources and information. It is a culturally grounded perception based on peoples' experiences with teachers and their understanding of teachers' professional roles. Such perception can last lifelong, but students must deliberately adjust and cope with the contextual definition of the teacher's role that facilitates their learning. Indeed, teachers' roles diverge from one context to another, which may bring supervision challenges to partners.

For example, I conversed with a professor, Jasmine, who commented on teachers as life-givers. She said,

"I could "biasedly inform that teachers are life-givers due to what most teachers have performed in my life and my community. I can reflect on my father, a teacher, and how he created lives for many children despite their parents' absence."

Jasmine is a professor and the child of a former teacher. Her father was a teacher under the British colony in one of the commonwealth countries, where education was an expensive commodity for a few. Although her society regarded teachers as life-givers, other commonwealth countries probably had different perspectives on teachers' positions. During colonialism in her community, education was for elites, so a few indigenous who could save the colonial leadership accessed formal education. The knowledge was also conveyed and shared in a foreign language, English, unknown to most parents. So, the system created a gap between the schools and the home where the two parties could not communicate.

3.1.3 Indigenous Learning System

The learning system dominated before the British emphasized learning by focusing on a specific profession. People learn through story-telling and practical work right from their childhood. The learning of a career was specific toward a particular area and assignment. For example, if someone were to become a housebuilder, they could start learning to build houses from childhood. Likewise, those who desired to fit in as caretakers could receive training for their duties early in their lives. Indeed, most women were prepared for caretaking roles. They mostly cared for families, including older people, children, and others, and girls learned how to perform such duties appropriately. They learned the caring task since childhood by observing how their mothers performed it and took small steps to perform the duties. In most cases, they could live with elderly grandmothers, observe the support they provided and received, and practice the same. They also collaborated with their mothers to provide the service required by those they care for and obtain feedback on their performance.

Contrary to female responsibilities, in most societies, men were mainly for outside-home duties such as farming, defense, and several other tasks. Others could learn how to tail clothes, carpets, and other home-use graphic arts items. Such practical learning was effective because children could instantly observe, learn/imitate, and practice while receiving feedback, corrections, and guidance. Learning by doing and solving contextual problems minimized the challenge of unemployment. Joblessness was not a vocabulary they knew of due to society's duty structure and practices, which allowed everyone to develop their talents and perform to their abilities.

The work of people who learn by doing is sometimes incomparable to those who graduate from the formal education system. For example, graduates in the social work and caring fields often read from different sources (López

(2020), Ford (2018)) about their weaknesses. Some practice cruelty to older and sick adults even though they know their dependency. Some older people experience difficulties from those they depend on for care, and some of today's caretakers are the product of the formal education system. Such social workers have a certificate indicating their capability for elderly and sick people care, but again, their education cannot adequately measure the level of passion and commitment.

Commonly, during the short time of their learning, which is two to three years, and the employment probation, most caretakers practice to the best of their abilities to obtain the trust they need from their assessors, not necessarily from the clients they save. Again, the caretakers and the elderly or sick person have no mutual communication and interest in each other in non-formal education. So, caretakers' education can make them valuable, and the one receiving care may be less useful depending on who is weaker. Physical, financial, and even social weaknesses influence the service provided to needy people. It implies that the education provided to the caretakers may sometimes not be adequate to qualify them.

If we refer to Jasmine, thus, Prof. Jasmine's father's devotion to supporting children and families was remarkable and unforgettable. However, I do not think his devotion came only from his education in the teaching college. Still, intrinsic motivation and passion for serving others drove him to perform such appreciative services. Teaching is a peculiar profession where people with a passion fit well and produce knowledgeable and skilled workforces for development. Moreover, the product of teachers' work can save local and international job markets.

Another person who informed me about formal education was one educator, Jacob. He told me that schools and community leaders in the old days, the early 1900s in his community, had to select children to join formal education intelligently in the colonial period. The selection mainly depended on their parents' services in the community and the children's understanding. For instance, religious leaders and politicians strongly influenced formal education provision, and their children were the primary consumers of education services. Although few people in the mentioned groups were educated, they knew the importance of formal education to themselves and society. They were easy to cope with the teachers, educational culture of foreign language and assignments.

Other factors that contributed to children's selection for formal education were parental awareness of the school system and their position in their communities. Parents who could communicate with teachers explaining their need for their children to join formal education had a better chance than the others. Usually, these parents knew how formal education could benefit their children and communities. Furthermore, although people were educated informally, the employment system focused on individual formal education attracted people to seek such money-based education. For instance, children from privileged families with known parents obtained learning positions over other groups due to their parents' awareness of education benefits. Besides, some parents were at decision-making desks and could favor the enrolment of their children.

Another factor that determined selection was the economic capabilities of the parents. In the old days, some parents in some societies were unable financially, and they were allowed to support schools in different ways to compensate for their financial limitations. For example, some could devote their time to supporting schools in physical work, such as building and ensuring their children were enrolled. Indeed, some schools obtained financial support from their governments to fulfill their learning objectives, and children were considered accordingly. The more government-supported schools, the more learners are admitted to schools. On the other hand, for children of people in need who demonstrated exceptional ability and talents, the heads of schools supported them to access education. Therefore, the school leadership had some power to decide who could join the school when they had vacancies.

Luckily, as a teacher, Jacob's father knew how important education was, and his understanding was a catalyst for Jacob to acquire formal education early and become a teacher. His father dealt with children of less privileged families, cleverly helping them access education after assessing their abilities. Due to his position, passion, and good name as a respectable community member, he could support others beyond the command of the colonial masters. Jacob informed that although his father regretted losing the indigenous practical teaching methods (learning by doing and talent evaluation), he allowed some indigenous content to penetrate the formal school curriculum in his district.

Therefore, Jacob's father worked beyond what the unpassionate teacher could do. He also organized other heads and parents to build schools without government support to increase their children's chances of obtaining formal education. Because the introduction of schooling went hand in hand with the spread of Christianity in their region, Sunday school teachers were also essential tools for identifying and selecting children for kindergarten and standard one. Indeed, the heads of schools collaborated with Sunday school teachers to evaluate children's reading and writing abilities. For example, children who could read and write Bible scriptures were allowed to join formal education regardless of their age. In addition, such children obtained new birthdays from the head of schools to access formal education.

Jacob said some parents did not even know their children's school age. Teachers' work was to ensure their pupils had the correct age groups required by the colonial masters. The only issue important to them was the ability of children to master the content taught at their education level. Indeed, teachers work for other peoples' children to support them to join and stay in formal education. Even though some parents had no financial connotes, the head of schools collaborated with other teachers to support the pupils.

Progressively, people lost the informal learning system they practiced before formal education. Those aware of the benefits associated with formal education had to find means to benefit from the new system. The cooperation and passion between and among teachers supported them in performing different learning tasks effectively to support learners.

Another lecturer, John, from another university and community, asserted,

"Supporting children to access formal education was conducted collaboratively by a group of heads of schools. They had to propose financial support to the children of less privileged families who could read and write to join formal education. The Secretary Ministry of Education's support was only for the few who received a strong recommendation from the schools' heads. Besides, not all who obtained a recommendation succeeded in joining formal education; other criteria contributed. However, mhh ... the endorsement of support to join formal education was the first step in the journey. These heads had to provide solid arguments for children to obtain government support, and they had to perform the task carefully ...."

He acknowledged the power of teachers, including the head of schools, in children's access to schooling. He also indicated the competition and the scarcity of education as one aspect that empowered teachers. Teachers assess, recommend, and teach the learners who obtained the school's endorsement, which results in enrollment.

Undeniably, some thought that the endorsement from the head of schools might resemble winning millions of dollars from the current Lotto money-winning game. Others may imagine how tempted people became to regard the head of schools and teachers as life-givers; some were just like that. They worked hard and by a passion for supporting learners to benefit from the formal education system. Moreover, teachers advocated for needy children, and their services to families and the community elevated them to a life benefactor position.

According to David, Jasmine, and Jacob's explanations, their father were examples of passionate and committed teachers. Furthermore, they informed me that (in the extended conversation with me) their communities had no memory of family complaining about teachers' conduct. Most teachers were committed, and the explanations from the mentioned educators have shown that devotion, commitment, and passion for learners' success are the essential attributes teachers should have acquired before joining the teaching profession. Indeed, many individuals and families can inform about teachers' practices. But unfortunately, some explanations have created the typical of what people think the role of teachers should be, and they assess them based on their perceptions. In addition, people's experience with teachers as learners or parents can create their perception of good or unprofessional teachers. For example, some individuals who have worked with teachers who were passionate and committed to learners can have a different mindset about teachers compared to those in the opposite circumstances.

Likewise, persons who work in a challenging learning environment that lacks the resources required for teaching and learning may demand that teachers' roles be different from those with adequate learning resources. In such circumstances, teachers may risk their pleasures by working beyond time expectations for learners to succeed. However, the less passionate teachers have no such attributes, especially in the current learning environments where teachers are appointed based on their academic performances and degree types. Indeed, some teachers allow themselves to be a ladder for their learners to climb and reach where they desire to go. Although some teachers remain in their position for many years, they do not tire of supporting learners to grow with determination. The majority becomes a foundation for learners to develop different knowledge and skills that benefit society. In most cases, committed teachers remain in their position while reinforcing learners to move on and take considerable societal responsibilities. For instance, some teachers may teach the same subjects for years, and employers often fail to promote or encourage them adequately. Still, they keep meeting their learners' anticipations and producing skilled laborers for different sectors. So, we can conclude that such committed and passionate teachers see beyond monetary benefits, thus fulfilling learners' interests, needs, and expectations.

As mentioned earlier, competent teachers tend to have intrinsic motivation and passion for finding and meeting learners' interests, needs, and expectations. It is the primary reason teaching should be a call and not a job because, without passion, one cannot fulfill learners' anticipations in a challenging environment. Moreover, in most cases, passionate teachers focus on students' successes even in demanding learning environments. I have seen people from institutions with learning deficits graduate with vital knowledge due to their teachers' devotion, commitment, and encouragement.

Therefore, Figure six insists on the three significant attributes of a competent teacher as a foundation for the teaching profession.

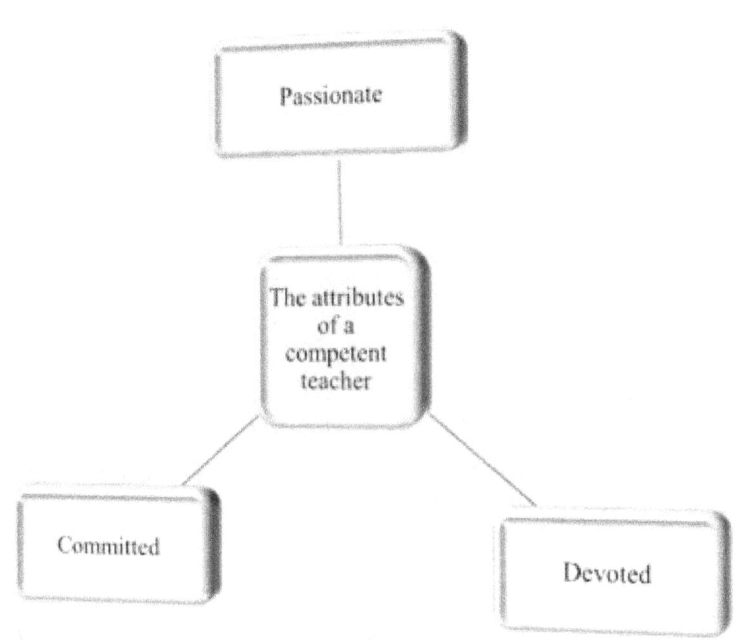

Figure 6. Attributes of a Competent Teacher

The figure indicates that passion, devotion, and commitment are the primary attributes required for a competent teacher at all levels of education. Lacking the mentioned attributes may lead one to fail to bear the challenges in the teaching profession. I will discuss these attributes in detail in another book because they are essential. Indeed, teachers' duties in eradicating ignorance are not limited to job descriptions but beyond like parents or a shepherd to the sheep. No one can adequately describe the work of teachers, and that is where teachers with the mentioned attributes fit to work more than their job requirements. Therefore, the principle of teachers' devotion, commitment, and passion applies to all levels of education. Let us discuss current teaching in postsecondary education in the next chapter.

Chapter 4

4.1 Teachers' Roles in Higher Education

In the previous chapter, I describe teachers' diverse roles and responsibilities. I also explain the complexity of the teaching profession and what it takes to be a good teacher. Indeed, teachers' duties are unique, and contextual learning circumstances often determine the roles and responsibilities of teachers. For example, during my conversation with some postsecondary students, I met with students with different experiences with teachers. The students had diverse descriptions of teachers' roles and responsibilities based on their experiences and culture. From their discussion, I realized that some think teachers' duties resemble caretakers of disabled persons, and they expect CARE when working with supervisors.

Others consider teachers as a doctor who can cure whatever disease engulf them. We all agree that ignorance is one of the fatal sicknesses that has killed many people's talents. Without a doubt, teachers who treat lack of knowledge as a disease may better understand their learners' problems and succeed in helping them become knowledgeable about the issue they desire to learn. Indeed, ignorance is a mental disability in knowledge and surely needs the right diagnosis and treatment to eradicate it. In normal circumstances, a sick person needs appropriate investigation that may lead to knowing the health problem and the right treatments to eliminate the illness, as does the ignorant person in education.

Fortunately, medical doctors have trained to listen to their patients carefully, comprehend their problems, and make the right diagnosis and treatment decisions. The doctor can do nothing with their expertise without understanding the patient's problem. For example, if it is difficult to recognize, he may use different tests to investigate and know the health trouble in the patient's body. It all starts by listening to the one who wants to be healthy, and the doctor keeps silent or asks questions. If you see a doctor who prescribes medicine without asking and listening to the patient, he must be unqualified.

I may share my experience with you about doctors' practices. One day, I was not feeling well and did not know the problem. So, I went to a nearby dispensary for a check-up, and a nurse referred me to a doctor. When I entered the consultation doctor's room, he bombarded me with questions and tried to figure out my health situation. He spent over half an hour asking fundamental questions to help him recognize the problem. After the questioning, he asked the nurse to take me to a laboratory for more investigation, where the nurse and the doctor collaboratively tested my blood and other bodily fluids. Eventually, they confirmed that I was not medically ill, even though I felt very weak. So, it ended up that I was not sick physically, and the doctor did not prescribe any medicine; rather, he advised resting and drinking adequate water. Although skeptical, I followed his advice and felt better and more energetic after three days. It was undoubtedly tiredness that made me feel the way I did.

Contrary, one of my friends with whom we were working on the same project was feeling horrible like me. So, she consulted a medical doctor near her home to find out what was wrong with her; it was not the same medical doctor I consulted, and although it was a male doctor, I gender him female to differentiate him from my doctor. Even though her medical doctor did not comprehend the problem, she quickly suspected that she might have encountered unpleasant food. So, she diagnosed her (without a laboratory check-up) food poisoning and prescribed medicine to reduce the poisoning and clear the blood. However, she used the medication for four days without feeling better, and her body became weaker and weaker.

Finally, she returned to the doctor on the fifth day of medication. The doctor proposed the change of the medicine to a stronger and more effective dose. However, my friend used the medicine for another four days without improvement and went to the doctor. Again, the doctor desired to change the medicine, but my friend asked her some questions that she could not answer, and that is when she left the dispensary for my home. She explained the story to me, and I asked her to consult my doctor, who went through the same procedure he took for me and concluded that she had no physical illness but fatigue. She was advised to rest and drink adequate liquids, especially water, and recovered after a few days.

Indeed, doctors' approach to their patients can be applicable in education between teachers and students, especially at the tertiary level, where research students learn individually with the consultation of their supervisors in a supervision fashion. The supervision partners usually sit in consulting rooms (offices, laboratories, restaurants, theatres, parks, etc.), discussing their projects and preparing strategies for research. So, as it is for doctors, supervisors need to listen to their students to comprehend their needs, expectations, and learning goals before strategizing the supervision methods to employ.

Moreover, supervisors cannot realize the resources required without understanding students' learning goals. Therefore, supervisors who do not investigate students' needs and expectations end with trial and error, resulting in student attrition. However, if the supervisor comprehends the student's ignorance area, conditions, and learning goals, he may propose the right resources. The investigation may also focus on utilizing resources effectively, eliminating obstacles, and strategizing to complete studies on time and successfully. It is vital to be clear about what students want to achieve because, as mentioned earlier, students have different needs and expectations. Thus, if the supervisor fails to understand students' learning needs and expectations, he should not guess or continue with supervision because it will not be successful; rather, he should call for another supervisor or rest.

Supervisors also have different ways of interacting with students to show respect, acceptance, and appreciation. In such a way, the supervisors become role models for students to learn to respect others, including supervisors. For example, one bachelor's student, Johnson, said he greatly admired teachers as "life-givers." He had such a mindset because of his experiences with teachers in primary and secondary schools. However, he studied postsecondary education in another region in the same country and observed different teachers' practices, making him doubt his perception of teachers' roles and divinities. He realized some teachers performed the teaching responsibilities for income and had no commitment or passion for helping students. The weaknesses of teachers made him not hold on to his previous beliefs of life-givers but evaluate each teacher individually based on their practices. In addition, the male student observed that some teachers were life-givers for a few students neglecting others.

I find his comments need attention and that education stakeholders should demand teachers' practices be scrutinized and assess their quality for students' success. Making follow-ups and evaluating teachers' approaches in the tertiary-level learning process may also support knowing and eradicating their challenges. For example, today, we talk about the policy of students' timely completion of degrees with little information on how the policy implementation has affected the learning process and outcomes. Yes, postsecondary teachers have written their frustration about the policy through literature but do not have experts to oversee their practices to come up with similar views. Lacking experts who monitor, control, and assess the work of postsecondary teachers, delays and sometimes overshadow in comprehending teachers' challenges and solving learning problems.

If we turn back to Johnson's experience, it means that the student had come across teachers who were not competent. Unfortunately, his experience is not new to many research students who have contacted undevoted teachers. Incompetent teachers are unaware of learners' learning objectives and do not expect successful results either. Moreover, some teachers are unwilling to work beyond the payment calculations because they lack passion. As a result, they are ineffective and have no qualifications and attributes required for the teaching profession. Worse enough, they do not admit their ineffectiveness nor seek support from other learning agencies. Instead, they camouflage their weaknesses by blaming students for not cooperating and regard them as unmotivated candidates.

In an extended conversation with Johnson, we discussed the teaching and learning of students in higher education. He was aware that the main aim of postsecondary teaching is to support students to be independent researchers and problem solvers. However, we could agree that students are not as knowledgeable as teachers at the beginning of their learning process, and they need support to acquire general knowledge before specific. Even students who introduce supervisors to their projects need guidance and information to support them in standing on other people's shoulders and meeting their needs while fulfilling the learning requirements.

For instance, students who have already formulated research projects, which may be out of the supervisors' area of study or unfamiliar to supervisors, still need supervisors' support to meet all the vital procedures. In addition, they need help to comprehend the resources available and accessible to their learning. Moreover, they need relevant information about diverse issues as a tool to act accordingly and perform as required. Of course, if students were competent to the level of their teachers, they could not need them, but they are ignorant in some areas. So, such students seek knowledge and skills to eradicate ignorance and require competent and passionate teachers to support them.

Certainly, some research students have observed teachers who do not care about their needs. It is a shame that these supervisors do not ask about students' expectations. It is an embarrassment that some universities hire unenthusiastic unqualified teachers and expect to produce skilled laborers. For example, teachers do not ask or comprehend their students' learning objectives. Likewise, they are not committed to their student's goals because they do not know them. They only work within the described working hours and tasks on supervision handbooks regardless of students' learning situation.

Nevertheless, like the doctors we discussed, teachers who do not ask students questions about their learning objectives indicate that they do not care about their students. Therefore, they cannot solve students learning problems, which is among the central aspects leading to student attrition. For instance, teachers who do not ask questions and are unaware of their student's "knowledge sickness" may prescribe inappropriate advice and publications, which cannot fulfill their learning goals.

As a result, the lack of commitment to students often becomes an obstacle to comprehending their strengths and weaknesses and the support they need. We can agree that without identifying the students' weaknesses, teachers become like doctors who prescribe medicine without knowing the patient's health issues. The supervisors' shortage of knowledge about students cannot help them properly guide them, and it is not an ethic expected from a good supervisor in postsecondary education. Committed, passionate, and devoted teachers aim to eliminate learners' knowledge sickness and develop their strengths, just as a good doctor needs to know the problem for the right diagnosis and treatment.

Understanding and dealing with learners' difficulties and fulfilling their anticipations is the essential task of a good teacher. Without assessing learners' vital learning objectives and aspects that facilitate or hinder their learning, it might be a challenge to support them successfully. Most of the time, teachers who teach blindly are like good drivers who drive people without knowing their destination. The drivers' expertise in driving cannot help until they move passengers to where they want to go. If they need to go west and drive them to the east, it will not be sensible, and they cannot appreciate his expertise. They would rather get out of the vehicle than leave the driver to drive them in the wrong direction because it does not meet their traveling objectives. Teaching without seeking learners' learning objectives, including needs, ability, project, and anticipations, and agreeing on the learning strategies may be a waste of resources, hence student attrition. So, Figure seven indicates the aspects vital for supervisors to focus on for learners' success.

Figure 7. Aspects to Focus on for Learners' Success

Figure seven suggests that teachers must focus on the specific and fundamental aspects of postsecondary students' success. Thus, students' learning objectives are the cornerstone for strategizing cooperation and the learning process. Moreover, the supervisor should ask questions that reveal students' weaknesses to help eradicate them. In addition, a competent teacher should regard students individually and comprehend their needs accordingly. Likewise, students' abilities should be a topic of interest for the supervisor to delegate some roles and responsibilities. In addition, the nature of the student's project should be known for resource allocation. Finally, the students and supervisors must communicate their expectations and create shared anticipations to facilitate cooperation. As mentioned earlier, failure to communicate these aspects with students indicates a lack of interest in students' success, hence an incompetent teacher/supervisor.

These factors are vital for research students' guidance so, I will discuss them again in the proceeding chapter.

Regrettably, some higher education and research supervisors are not interested in comprehending learners' objectives and destinations but in fulfilling the implementation of institutional and governmental policies. For example, as mentioned earlier, the primary policy determinant in higher education is the student's timely degree completion. Meaning the students are supposed to complete their studies within a specific timeframe. The primary implementers of the policy are teachers and students in higher education, and they better understand the effect of the policy on learning. Some teachers have written about the policy, and their concerns are in different publications.

Similarly, scholarly literature has shown that timely completion pressure has become one reason that has led to student attrition in most higher education institutions (Urassa, 2021,2022). Indeed, students do not drop out because of the policy, but the practices surrounding its implementation have changed the supervision. It has caused communication between the partners difficult, and they have no adequate time to observe the aspects discussed in the previous section. Indeed, the implementation has caused more stress than the one experienced during the fault-finding school inspection. Even though no one makes follow-ups in research students' supervision practices, the supervisors in some universities are promoted or maintain their employment based on the students' graduations statistic. The more supervisors produce or support students in completing their studies, the better their employment position and quality.

Therefore, higher education teachers' assessments reflect the student's graduation. The learning process is less emphasized, and students drop out of the research learning journey because, among others, supervision objectives contradict their needs. The supervisors desire their students to complete their studies timely, even if unsuccessful. The main motive has become to fulfill their employers' or owners of the institution's desires regardless of students' learning conditions (refer to figure seven). Thus, most attrition is caused by supervisors' failure to lead students to meet their learning needs and expectations. Instead of taking them where they desire to go, they are directing them to an unexpected path, just as the professional driver I mentioned. During the implementation of the policy, diverse challenges may occur; whether the problem arises in the discussion, research task, or relationships, the supervisors should be partly responsible because they are research student leaders.

As we have discussed concerning inspection/supervision in lower levels, we have observed that the inspectors were focusing on the process of learning. Indeed, the processes students and teachers undertake in learning support students in acquiring and developing diverse skills. For example, learners may develop communication, interpersonal, writing, and other skills in the learning process. In addition, some students acquire vital social skills to cope with multicultural and interdisciplinary learning environments. As mentioned, some people join higher education and research degrees not for quick graduation but to enjoy the process, communicate with others, learn the culture, and eventually graduate. Thus, completing the degree timely without enjoying the process may not be the objective for many research students; hence, the learning journey with supervisors emphasizing merely timely completion may become challenging.

4.1.1 Dream Killers Supervisors

In the previous chapter, I discussed the perspective that teachers are life-givers. The explanation focused on teachers' roles and responsibilities for years and how they construct and produce knowledgeable and skilled individuals. However, some people and research students with negative teacher experiences have diffcrent perspectives. They can explain their stories by demonstrating teachers as dream killers or life-takers. Some students have dropped out of their studies because they meet with such dream killers' supervisors. The dream killers do not understand students' interests, needs, and expectations. Instead, they impose rules and procedures that the students must observe even before comprehending the aspects in Figure seven.

For instance, instead of supervisors discovering students' problems and diagonalizing to find a proper treatment, they become like my friend's doctor. They work hard to demonstrate their expertise while ignoring students' needs and expectations. In addition, some threaten the students and oppress them to suppress students' desire to complain about their weaknesses. Finally, the dream killers may do all they can to ensure students' voices are nowhere except where they choose. They even sabotage students in many ways that no one can comprehend because there is no monitoring and evaluation of their practices. And unfortunately, some students have no culture of opposing, challenging, and questioning the work of teachers.

Indeed, many practices from teachers indicate weakness in knowing students' needs and oppression. For example, some research students have experienced sexual harassment and other abusive practices from their teachers. Scholarly literature has informed of such practices at all levels, mostly in higher education. For example, publications by Rivers & Duncan (2013), Wood, Hoefer, Kammer-Kerwick, Parra-Cardona & Busch-Armendariz (2021), and Clarke (2021) explain the challenge that exists in higher education associated with sexual harassment where students are taken advantage of by their supervisors.

One may also expand his knowledge on sexual harassment in higher education by reviewing literature by Clarke (2021), Faulkner & Adams (2021), and Cahn (Ed.) (2021). In addition, Karami, Spinel, White, Ford & Swan (2021)) have discussed the unacceptable sexual experiences students encounter in their learning which may hinder them from attaining their learning goals. Therefore, most people and higher education students have unpleasant stories concerning teachers that describe their perception of teachers' roles differently from life-giving individuals.

Likewise, some teachers are dream killers because teaching is a job, focusing on increasing their earnings while neglecting learners' needs and anticipations. For example, such supervisors overload themselves with money-generating research projects that hinder them from supervising research students. Others engage in excessive writing for money and their activities conflict with the teaching assignments. Consequently, such teachers are not committed to students learning and have no passion for teaching. Similarly, they do not consider the rewards associated with helping learners to eradicate their ignorance and society obtaining knowledgeable and skilled laborers as essential. Unfortunately, these uncommitted and unpassionate teachers have no one to monitor their practices to ensure students learning. As a result, they go free from accusations even when they kill students' dreams and society's investments.

If we refer to David's story, although he is a professor today, after his bachelor's degree graduation, he became a teacher in secondary school like his father. He devoted himself to meeting students' needs and expectations every day of his teaching. At first, he taught biology and chemistry; later, due to the shortage of teachers in secondary schools in his region, he had to teach all subjects. Finally, after some years of teaching, he became a school inspector, evaluating and supporting other teachers with teaching techniques. David said it was not hard to see the differences between the committed teachers and dream killers.

Professor David described dream killers as those who do not prepare for their teaching sessions. Such teachers teach on top of their students' heads and do not consider their actions to affect students' learning. They usually do not ask students relevant questions to determine their interests, needs, and expectations. In addition, the dream killers have no strategies to improve their teaching or even discuss their plans with students. Often, they have different expectations from their students and never create shared learning expectations. His explanation aligns with what my informants described as qualities of incompetent supervisors.

The university teacher, Prof. David, liked his teaching calling, and he could declare and agree with the motto, "Teaching is a Call, not a Job." He believed that the teaching profession is a burden without a call, and it is not advisable for anyone to join the work if not his call. One may also advise good teachers not to change their teaching professions to others because when a life-giver change to another career is a loss to many learners. Yes, jobs with more money and prestige than teaching may attract teachers. However, the most rewarding, recognized, and appreciated professions are those that care for people and solve their problems, and teaching is one of them. Therefore, before a supervisor who thinks she is a life-giver change the profession, she must put herself in the learners' position. Teachers who believe in learners keep teaching and formulating new teaching strategies, while dream killers keep changing institutions and jobs. So, the best thing teachers should do is understand their intention to join the profession and work to improve their learners.

Undoubtedly, learners have diverse demands that need to be known. They can gradually communicate with passionate and committed teachers who pay attention, show interest, and are willing to help; without these attributes, learners may not open up adequately. And if supervisors are not aware of students' interests, needs, and expectations, they cannot meet them. Professor David's explanation of the teaching profession was exciting and should remind higher education teachers of the required qualities. Honestly, the primary responsibility of a teacher with the attributes mentioned, regardless of the level of education and availability of information and other resources, is to comprehend the aspects in Figure seven. Equally important is collaborating with students in formulating shared expectations while strategizing to fulfill them.

However, as we have seen, there are dream killers who do not observe the aspects mentioned. Indeed, teachers' conduct and practices must be scrutinized, debated, and challenged regardless of their roles and learners' level of education. Teachers are undoubtedly essential in producing knowledgeable and skilled laborers globally. A knowledgeable and professional workforce is critical in human development, and the task requires monitoring, measuring, and evaluating teachers' practices. Likewise, we have seen that in higher education and research degree, students and supervisors are the implementers of the policy of timely completion, and they have diverse responsibilities that may hinder them from fulfilling teaching duties. Therefore, the lack of monitoring and evaluation of supervisors' practices in higher education has become a new corona-killing students' degrees worldwide. So, it is an excellent time to re-think higher education supervision which supports supervisors and students in charge for better student learning processes and outcomes.

4.1.2 Students as Teachers' Life-givers

There are challenges in tertiary education because some institutions claim that students are teachers' assessors. However, their assessment is partial, even when students are encouraged to be equal to their supervisors. For instance, many universities preach that research students, primarily Ph.D. are supervisors' companions. They claim that students have equal rights as their supervisors in expressing themselves and demanding the fulfillment of their learning goals. The first measure these universities have taken is to ask students to evaluate their teachers. Student evaluation has been a typical practice university apply to demonstrate equality. It is debatable whether the institution's management uses the results in decision-making. Certainly, it may be that some universities use the result to promote teachers, terminate their contracts, or assign them other responsibilities, but little has to change the supervision system.

Therefore, regardless of students' assessment, they cannot adequately evaluate teachers' abilities because they are not experts. Moreover, their evaluation may be biased if they do not receive guidance and understand the contextual perception of the roles and responsibilities of teachers. Besides, students have diverse perspectives on the quality of good teachers that may conflict with each other and the host institution's philosophy. As a result, some teachers have become frustrated with students' evaluations because they do not consistently demonstrate their effort or weaknesses to students.

Some universities take students' evaluations seriously, and students receive forms with questionnaires to respond to concerning their teachers. So, yes, students' assessment has become crucial, and the results are considered part of the qualities assessment of teachers and applied in ranking universities. However, scholars such as Husbands & Fosh (1993), Chen & Hoshower (2003), and Spooren, Mortelmans & Denekens (2007) have written about the students' roles and responsibilities in assessing their teachers. Likewise, some have indicated unreliability and challenge for such evaluation, such as Spooren, Brockx & Mortelmans (2013) and Hillman Tandberg & Fryar (2015).

The scholars revealed that using students' assessments of their teachers in formative and summative evaluation can be problematic. They focus on the diverse opinion of a good teacher and students' inexperience with learning culture in higher education. In addition, many higher education stakeholders are skeptical about trusting students' evaluation, among others, because of the position (life-givers) teachers have had for ages in education. Moreover, the diverse student perceptions of the roles of supervisors play a part in doubting students' evaluation of teachers, significantly when their previous experience influences their decisions.

Indeed, the scholarly arguments are crucial in understanding the power shift from teachers to students, but it may help to think that students' evaluation is insufficient in evaluating supervisors' quality. Indeed, one may argue that student assessments of their teachers may be biased and unprofessional because they lack adequate knowledge in monitoring and assessing supervision. Thus, students' perceptions of a good supervisor diverge from each other, which may challenge their evaluation.

For instance, one doctoral degree student, Ashura, contended:

"Teachers in this University are just like anybody else; we criticize them, and sometimes we work together harmoniously. We have never thought that they are above the rules and that they can terrorize students. Besides, we evaluate our teachers every semester; their weaknesses can be identified soon and discussed with the teachers in supervision sessions, and sometimes we talk with other advisors. Students with different problems communicating with their teachers tend to report the case to the university leadership, such as the dean of students ...."

Ashura's explanation indicates a power shift. The student may have liberal ideas demonstrating a decrease in teachers' status. However, students' power to assess their teachers is significant step universities have taken to show the necessity of monitoring and evaluating teachers' work. They have seen the significance of getting information on teachers' practices in learning and whether they meet students learning goals. Moreover, it demonstrates that teachers need someone to watch their work and report to their employers. Finally, it is a change of responsibilities because students had no power to assess their teachers in the old days. Still, now they do, and their evaluation affects the institution's quality, teachers' employment, and funding accordingly.

Nevertheless, scholarly literature has reported that students tend to be biased in their evaluation. For example, Greimel-Fuhrmann & Geyer (2003); Spooren, Mortelmans & Denekens (2007) said that students' assessment is vital for quality learning. Nonetheless, it depends on students' understanding of their teachers' teaching duties and how they relate to the teachers and the subjects. They also informed that students' mindset toward evaluation influences their assessment significantly. For instance, the review of teachers that aims at improving learning and choice, of course, its outcomes may differ from those required for teachers' promotion and employment. Some think students' bias cannot last long, and students are not permanent assessors; rather, they complete their studies, and the new bunch may disclose weaknesses.

Ashura continued,

"Although some HEIS administrators are skeptical about students' assessment, I believe it is essential for any institution to acquire this evaluation system where students express their satisfaction in learning and teaching. Some of the allegations ... provided by administrators who doubt the students assess that mhh ... they think popular teachers who have created a friendship with students receive positive recommendations from students even though they are not competent in teaching and researching ...."

Like many students, Ashura thinks the assessment is vital, and she does not believe students' judgments may be biased or teachers' popularity may influence students' decisions for a long time. It will not last long if teachers' popularity is the case without academic performance. So, she believed that administrators must trust students in their evaluation of teachers.

Indeed, the assessment conducted by students in most HEIs is vital, but it is debatable whether it is relevant for professional continuation and promotions or quality of learning (Darwin (2017), Spooren, Mortelmans & Denekens (2007)). Undeniably, the change in the education system and higher education has altered teachers' position, and in some institutions, students have become life-givers to their teachers.

Consequently, the institutions which apply student evaluation for employment and promotion of teachers have legitimated students to be life-givers to their teachers. However, employers must be careful relying on such evaluation because, as mentioned earlier, students inform the quality of teaching based on their perceptions of the roles of teachers and whether teachers meet students' expectations.

Scholars such as Wadesango & Machingambi (2011), Pyhältö & Keskinen (2012), Yousefi, Bazrafkan & Yamani (2015), Kaur, Kumar, & Noman (2021), Grant (2005, 2008) explain the challenges students and supervisors encounter in supervision. Therefore, if the partners have challenges comprehending their roles, responsibilities, and expectations, they might have difficulties evaluating their performances. The encounter with students' evaluation is how their previous experiences with teachers influence their judgment and the training to prepare them for their assessment. As I stated earlier, people perceive teachers' roles differently based on their cultural beliefs and experiences. Thus, their perceptions may affect the evaluation if some regard teachers as life-givers and others as dream killers.

Scholars have not supported students' evaluation of their teachers as a solution for monitoring supervisors. For instance, Saroyan & Amundsen (2001), when dealing with teaching evaluation and ranking of institutions, asserted; that students lack evaluation skills, and their diverse concept of teachers' roles may pose challenges in supervision and quality evaluation.

Likewise, Wisker (2005), focusing on the UK, explained the difficulties of supervising international students, including cultural and conceptual differences in learning. Other scholars have explained the issue of students' backgrounds and the challenges imposed in understanding teachers' responsibilities. Among them are Grant and Pearson (2007), Lee (2007), Grant & Manathunga (2011), and Kimani (2014), who connected diversity and challenges in supervision. So, it shows that students' cultural background plays a vital role in comprehending the parts of higher education teachers, and that affects evaluation.

Undeniably, students' fairness is uncertain, although letting students assess their teachers is a positive sign of necessity for monitoring and evaluating teachers' practices. Students' empowerment in higher education is one of the traditions that have emerged because students comprehend better what is happening behind the closed doors of the supervision venue. However, the majority have not received assessment courses that could ensure the reliability and validity of their assessment. Nevertheless, we should not forget that many students lack the knowledge and skills to assess teachers' quality.

Indeed, the evaluation of higher education teachers should be performed by experts who comprehend teachers' and students' general and specific roles and responsibilities. Besides, people aware of different stages in research learning and requirements in supervision may be more appropriate assessors. Therefore, establishing a supervision unit in universities where experienced professors may monitor and evaluate the supervisors' work can benefit all stakeholders.

According to the explanation provided demonstrating teachers' qualifications, attributes, and roles, we may conclude that teachers are the cornerstone for students' success at all levels of education. Indeed, they have several responsibilities of supporting learners in different stages and dimensions of their learning. Furthermore, most learners have other interests, needs, abilities, and expectations that some teachers cannot fulfill adequately. The students' diversity in teachers' roles and responsibilities affects their assessment of the quality of teachers. In addition, most students lack the knowledge and skills required to review teachers' work objectively.

On the contrary, we also know that scholars are not satisfied with students' evaluations of their teachers, and the practice is under debate. At the same time, we have seen the need for monitoring and evaluating teachers' work at all levels of education. It is believed that teachers whose practices are often monitored and assessed may become more effective than the opposite. However, the roles of teachers are influenced by many factors, including the resources, students' abilities, the nature of students' projects, needs, and expectations. Therefore, contextual monitoring and evaluating teachers' practice can bring effectiveness to students learning and fulfilling their needs and expectations.

In the next chapter, I will attempt to discuss the general roles of teachers that most people globally look up to.

Chapter 5

5.1 Global Roles of Teachers

This section will discuss the role of teachers in higher education, meaning supervisors of research degree students. It has been challenging to comprehend the supervision process adequately. Often the experiences differ from one student to another and a supervisor to another. The complexity of research learning has increased with implementing a timely degree completion policy without adequate guidance to implementers. However, the policy is vivid, and its success depends on teachers' understanding of research students' needs, interests, and expectations. It also depends on the availability and accessibility of vital resources (human and material) and the nature of the projects. Equally crucial for teachers to observe when supervising are their understanding of the requirements and communication with students. Therefore, teachers who comprehend these aspects early in supervision may support students adequately and successfully within the timeframe, and the opposite is the case.

The practical procedure for students to obtain supervisors in higher education varies. Typically, a research student is assigned at least two supervisors to oversee their work and provide feedback. Most doctoral students tend to communicate with the academics before admission and know their supervisors before enrolling. Thus, some institutions allow students to choose supervisors, and others have no such liberal practice. However, after the student has obtained the supervisors, by her choice or provision, the partners (a student and supervisors) should observe guidance in the institutional supervision handbook, which usually consists of supervision rules and regulations. So, the partners may agree on the structure and practice they should apply and the activities required in each supervision session. However, their agreement is unofficial and between them without follow-ups from a third party (inspectors or other officials). Sometimes, the arrangements between them and their relationships remain unknown to the institution's leadership until they have a dispute. The misunderstandings are the significant source of many revelations in supervision, where partners demonstrate their experiences and challenges working together.

As mentioned earlier, teachers have diverse roles depending on many factors surrounding the institution and the students. First, the institution's development in terms of availability and accessibility of resources significantly influences teachers' functions. The more the institution has sophisticated resources accessible to students and academics, the lower the roles of teachers in assisting students with reading materials. For example, teachers will not have to prepare references for the research students if the university has up-to-date publications. Instead, they will inform students where to obtain the materials and the specific scholars they should focus on. After that, the students may work independently, with peers, or with other learning agencies.

Indeed, the accessibility of resources facilitates student learning in many ways. In many cases, teachers will provide guidance and involve themselves in students' learning where their support is needed only. Students may also turn to their supervisors mainly for clarifications or comprehensive information. Thus, students may deal with different assignments without consulting their teachers because they have adequate resources. Sometimes, the students may obtain only essential advice and support while increasing their independence. Remember, research training aims to produce independent researchers who can solve society's problems scientifically. Therefore, students' independent learning habits are needed to support them in becoming autonomous and learning to create new knowledge using the available resources. However, the resources may sometimes be inadequate, affecting students' learning negatively if they do not obtain significant support from their supervisors.

Again, teachers in most resourceful institutions, their lectures and advice may be available online for students to access at their convenience. Therefore, students wanting to learn something before contacting their supervisors may consult online courses. In addition, such institutions have up-to-date generic learning programs where students can access the necessary information without consulting their supervisors. For example, if a student needs to comprehend rules and deadlines, regulations, or course enrolment deadlines, he may obtain information online. Students may also need to understand how to deal with literature review or data analysis and find reliable and valuable information online. However, sometimes it is beneficial to discuss the information with teachers to clarify ambiguities and provide contextual interpretations.

To access information online, students need to log on to a computer. Therefore, computers are another resource required for research degree students to succeed. However, students in most sophisticated higher education institutions access computers and the internet for online publications and other necessary information. Usually, students acquire a username and password for the accessibility of online learning information on university computers. Some universities have restrictions on the accessibility of computers, but most universities allow students to use computers within the campus regardless of the department. Still, few universities provide students with laptops to be more flexible so they can work at their convenient time and space. As a new research student, one should check with the responsible people on the resources and their access to different areas. The knowledge may help them comprehend the procedures and regulations required.

Consequently, the primary resource students need in their learning is publications. Higher education learning requires a literature review from the beginning, where the students investigate the knowledge gap to fill the end. So, they must read widely to critique and discover the area they desire to engage in to bring awareness or solve problems. Online literature is a norm in many universities to supplement physical library publications. Most students find it beneficial to deal with online and physical literature as it provides a wide range of selections. Thus, one may find a variety of literature from books, journals, theses, and articles in audio, video, and images. In addition, students in sophisticated universities often have access to online examinations, archives, educative television channels, and radio to inform them about various topics.

In this case, teachers are responsible for guiding students in selecting relevant literature for their project and providing recommendations on what to review. In addition, some universities conduct seminars and workshops assisting students in dealing with diverse issues in their learning process, including dealing with literature. Other universities discuss literature availability, accessibility, and review in the orientation programs with first years. It does not matter the level of education or degree students has enrolled in, but all first years may obtain essential information concerning the institution's structure and practices, including literature.

Even though some seminars and workshops are designed by non-academic personnel, they tend to have the competencies to lead students accordingly. Hence the supervisors whose students have adequate information about literature have little to do in supporting students in this area. Nevertheless, the universities which lack such programs and with a shortage of resources, including online publications, their supervisors have more duties to perform to support students.

So, the accessibility of information and other learning resources affects the supervisors' tasks and frequency of meetings with students. Therefore, for most experienced supervisors, the primary task is to inform students of the available and accessible resources. Further, the teachers support students in obtaining supporting agencies and appropriately utilizing resources. Sometimes, the teacher may connect students with materials and agencies that can assist them with advice. For example, laboratory technicians, computer assistants, and librarians usually help students with diverse technical issues. Besides, the more students have connected to other learning agencies apart from their supervisors, the more they widen their network, learn about diverse topics from various departments, and the less the task of their teachers. Therefore, some supervisors purposively support students to connect with other learning agencies in their institutions and beyond.

Besides the institutional state, the supervisors' tasks depend on students' capability in research learning and the field. Thus, the more students master the information, procedures, and protocols concerning the learning structure and practices, the lower the supervisors' responsibilities. For instance, students who can write a research proposal with little supervisor support will not spend many hours in meetings or receiving instructions. They will engage with tasks without supervisors' close guidance and may utilize their time more effectively, focusing on specific issues in supervision. Such students comprehend the area they need supervisors' assistance, and when in meetings, they direct their conversation to meet their needs. However, students with a low ability to identify their needs may waste time waiting for supervisors' instructions.

All in all, students' ability is essential to be known by the supervisors. If the supervisor understands the student's ability, it helps to determine his tasks. Indeed, for the supervisor to comprehend the student's ability, they must communicate their duties and resources. The communication should be meaningful for the partners to create shared expectations. On the other hand, revealing the roles and sharing responsibilities may uncover students' capabilities in many areas, including research. Afterward, the partners may agree on cooperation and attend to their inquiries while attaining their expectations.

Another issue determining the supervisors' engagement is the nature of the project. If a student joins the supervisors' project, they have several issues to inform and guide the student compared to students who have formulated research projects by themselves. Supervisors should first introduce the student to the project and provide vital information, including the project objectives and significance. Second, the supervisors should persuade the student to review relevant documents concerning the project to gain more knowledge and assist her in comprehending and evaluating its effectiveness. Third, the supervisor ought to support the student in understanding the position of other delegates in the project and guiding her in associating with relevant people. Fourthly, to help the student understand her situation and responsibilities in the project and the limits and delimitations related to her position.

However, supervisors may have a few of the many responsibilities when a student introduces them to her project. In such a case, the student might be more knowledgeable about the project than the supervisor, which can support the student in continuing.

Moreover, the student should communicate her needs with the supervisor. Research students have different needs, especially where some have disabilities that may hinder them from working with the available facilities in the learning context. They may need some modification of the learning environment or types of equipment to cope with daily learning. Such needs call for fulfillment for the student to learn in a conducive environment and be productive. For example, students may need special computer items, a room, publications (for blind people), and the like. Supervisors are responsible for discussing students' needs from the beginning of their cooperation and supporting them in finding solutions. The discussion on the needs should go hand in hand with the learning objectives and expectations. The more students clarify their expectations and understand their learning objectives, the easier attaining them becomes.

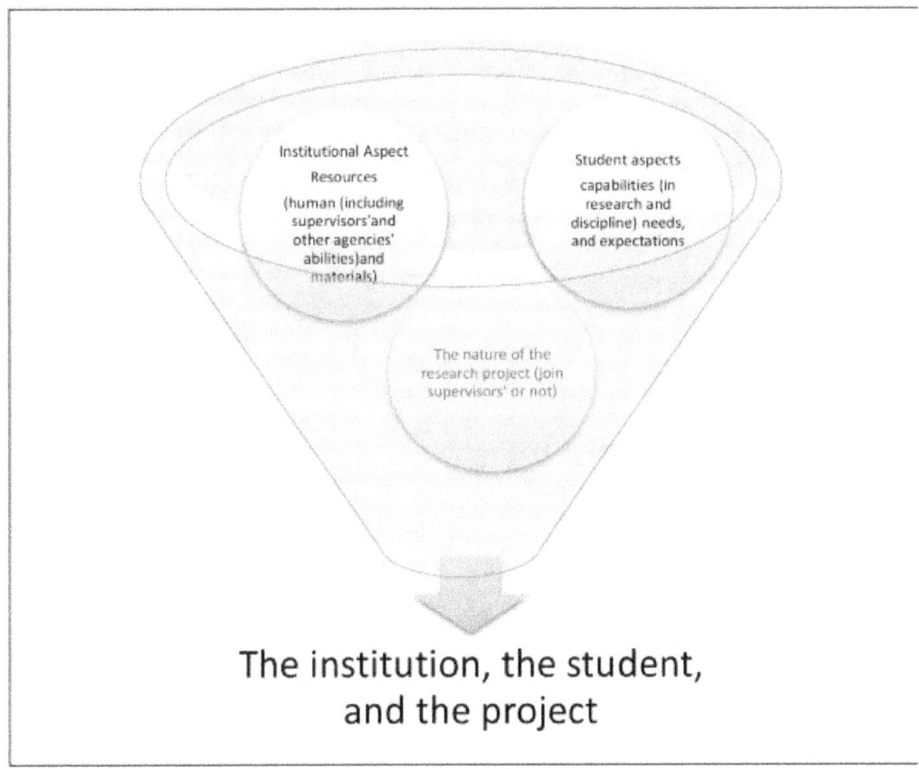

Figure 8. Determinants of Supervisors' Duties

Figure eight indicates that the primary factors are in three categories. First, the institutions' status in terms of availability and accessibility of resources, both human and physical, determine the duties of a teacher. Second, the nature of the project (new to the student or new to the supervisor) is another determinant of the supervisors' responsibilities. Finally, the factors within the student, such as the ability, needs, and expectations, can influence supervisors' duties.

Indeed, millions of factors may influence supervisors' duties, but most fall into the three mentioned categories: institution, student, and project. Therefore, since the availability and accessibility of learning resources differ from one institution to another, so do the teachers' duties. Again, the student's abilities and the nature of their projects differ and may require different resources that may also alter the work of supervisors. So, the variation in resources and ability legitimate the diversity in teachers' roles and responsibilities worldwide. Thus, students must learn the practices of the three factors mentioned in this chapter in their institutions to determine the work of their supervisors. Comprehending the tasks performed by supervisors may also help students predict theirs. However, although teachers' duties fall into the mentioned three categories, students should be curious to comprehend the contextual definition of the role and responsibilities of teachers.

5.1.1 Contextual Teachers' Roles

The previous section discusses the general roles of teachers in higher education. This section will deal with the specific roles of higher education teachers, which vary from one department, institution to another, and society to others. As mentioned earlier, the responsibilities of teachers depend mainly on resources, students' capabilities, needs, and expectations. It also depends on the nature of the research projects and their objectives. Therefore, the mentioned aspects are the essential determinants of supervisors' roles in higher education learning environments.

Previously, we also discussed the tendency of students to transfer their perceptions of teachers' roles from one context to another and the challenges they may create in such practice. However, the qualities of teachers are measured differently from one environment to another and transferring the measurement can fail to demonstrate reality. Therefore, research students need to be observant and investigate whether their understanding of teachers' roles is relevant and aligns with their contextual learning environment. This chapter may help give students suggestions on comprehending specific and contextual teachers' roles and responsibilities.

First, they must investigate the resources available and accessible to students. Indeed, the more resources available and accessible to students, the fewer the supervisors' tasks and the more independent students should become. Second, they must comprehend the rule applied when resources are adequate; thus, students learn with minimal supervisor support in such an environment. Third, most of the time, students search for knowledge by themselves and have diverse learning sources and support from others than their supervisors. Therefore, if a student enrolls in a university equipped with sufficient resources required for learning and has access to the resources, he cannot expect spoon-feeding from supervisors. Instead, the student must realize that becoming independent and utilizing the available resources is the most vital ability they should acquire and express. Of course, it does not mean the supervisors will not engage, but the student must use the resources and stop turning to the supervisors for every solution.

Furthermore, students can comprehend the roles of teachers by examining their contributions to their projects. Thus, teachers' contributions to students' projects may support assessing their roles, and the more they contribute, the more they indicate their understanding and interest in students' projects. For example, if the students join supervisors' projects, they may carry different roles than students who introduce supervisors to their projects. The students who have planned their project might have reviewed adequate literature and sketched the plan and strategies to fill the knowledge gap. They probably do not need supervisors' close supervision or frequent meetings like those who join unfamiliar projects.

In addition, the way supervisors communicate with students and their position in society can inform their roles. Supervisors who demonstrate an authoritative leadership style indicate power over students, which may lie in the resources and information. In most institutions with adequate learning resources, the supervisors tend to be democratic and hesitate to give instruction and decide for students. They have acquired such behavior because, among others, students tend to have access to resources that may provide them with relevant, up-to-date information equally as supervisors. Students may be more knowledgeable than their supervisors in some areas, which can change their communication altogether.

Therefore, supervisors in learning contexts where resources are available and accessible tend to cooperate with students instead of controlling them. In addition, supervisors tend to ask questions rather than confidently respond to students' inquiries. In general, the communication and leadership style in supervision shifts with the availability and accessibility of resources. As a result, students unfamiliar with contextual learning resource situations may be confused when the supervision practice changes from their expectations. Therefore, it is better to understand that supervisors typically create democratic and independent learning in an environment with adequate, relevant resources. However, in an environment with limited information and insufficient learning resources, especially where students have no equal access to supplies, supervisors tend to withdraw democratic and independent learning.

Sometimes, teachers can disclose their role through their actions when teaching or consulting students. For example, they may utilize a supervision handbook to clarify their duties and help students know their roles while demonstrating the scope of their cooperation. Although the supervision handbooks cannot inform the type of relationship students and supervisors should have, some supervisors describe the expected relation apart from ethical ones. Therefore, understanding the supervisors' relational limitations and delimitations in supervision and responsibilities is essential and beneficial for students. Indeed, students need to comprehend their roles, and if they are against supervisors' expectations, a discussion may be the way to deal with the ambiguities. Both students and supervisors have relational expectations that each other must comprehend for their cooperation to be effective and productive.

One student informed me that his supervisor expected her to be his girlfriend. He was doing all he could to believe that, and finally, she realized later that the supervisor was genuinely doing his job by being kind to her. Of course, the male supervisor had no intention of such relation, but the student had illusive relational expectations. The more relational misunderstandings occur in supervision, the more indication that one or both partners have not known their roles and responsibilities. Therefore, discussing the appropriate relationship and agreeing on limitations can solve this problem and facilitate harmony in supervision.

Another way of comprehending teachers' roles is to read written information on the university web pages. For instance, most universities have information about their faculties and departments, including a list of supervisors and their roles and responsibilities. One may review the sites and comprehend the supervisors' responsibilities, projects, and outside academia. Some may have different functions apart from supervision and teaching; therefore, understanding their diverse responsibilities in and outside the university can support students in predicting their commitment and availability for supervision tasks. As a rule, the more supervisors' non-academic responsibilities increase, the less time they have for supervision, and vice versa, maybe the truth. However, some balance their academic and non-academic roles and responsibilities by delegating their duties to support students.

In addition, universities provide students and supervisors with a supervision handbook consisting of the roles and responsibilities of each party. Although, as I mentioned earlier, the book informs mainly of rules and regulations, it also provides the boundaries of supervisors' partners' duties. Furthermore, it reminds the partners of the discipline required in their cooperation and the step to take whenever they face challenges. Again, no neutral or independent organs or individuals deal with misunderstandings between the students and supervisors in supervision. However, reading the supervision handbook can support students in comprehending their supervisors' duties and theirs.

Another method to apply when finding the specific roles of supervisors is to contact the relevant sources of information, thus, academic advisors. Most of the time, student graduate advisors may save the purpose of elaborating on teachers' contextual roles and responsibilities. However, some universities have several advisors for postgraduate students who may have helpful information about teachers and their roles. When students enroll in a university, they sometimes meet with graduate institutional advisors before meeting their academic supervisors. The primary function of advisors is to inform students of vital issues and respond to students' inquiries. The common topic in such meetings may be to educate students on their rights and obligations in learning and beyond. In addition, one may use the opportunity to discuss teachers' duties and guide students to comprehend their expectations.

Another way to obtain helpful information concerning teachers' responsibilities is to discuss the matter with them. For example, research students, especially those with doctoral degrees, meet their supervisors before other learning agencies after enrolment. The three initial supervision meetings are essential to make things right and understand the scope of teachers' duties. Students need to consult with their supervisors while clarifying the role and responsibilities of each other in supervision. Students can also inform their experiences associated with teachers' responsibilities to avoid confusion caused by assumptions. At the same time, the discussion may educate students about supervisors' contextual expectations of students and allow students to criticize the perceptions. Such dyadic conversation can be vital in clearing partners' ambiguities concerning their roles and responsibilities and eliminating unrealistic anticipations.

Whatever the case, higher education students must be curious to understand teachers' contextual roles and responsibilities. Indeed, students who desire to comprehend the appropriate supervision structure and teachers' practices in their learning may be successful compared to others. Moreover, it is essential to understand teachers' duties to predict students' roles and responsibilities and determine whether they align with each other's expectations. Besides, students cannot evaluate the quality of their teachers if they do not comprehend their duties in learning. The extent to which they understand teachers' duties facilitates fulfilling their roles and responsibilities.

Thus, the explanation of teachers' duties diversity justifies that students must not rely on their previous experiences, perceptions, and practices because they may differ from the contextual definitions and procedures. Indeed, assumptions and misunderstandings concerning the roles and responsibilities of supervisors can cause several problems that may damage supervision relationships, delay students' completion, and cause attrition. Therefore, people must investigate teachers' duties before commencing or enrolling in the institution of their choice. The information may determine the kind of service students obtain, and one can evaluate his expectations realistically while allowing the roles of teachers to be the catalyst for their decisions. Indeed, comprehending teachers' duties in supervision is the foundation of successful cooperation and students' graduation.

Undoubtedly, there are many ways of understanding the contextual roles of teachers, but the mentioned can save the purpose. If students do not comprehend the contextual teachers' roles and responsibilities by applying the mentioned strategy, they must be creative and find other methods. The big mistake is for students to supervise without clearly understanding the teachers' duties.

Table 1. How to Comprehend Supervisors' Roles

How to understanding the contextual roles of teachers/supervisors						
Observe their leadership style	Read the university webpages	Consult the supervision handbook	Ask Graduate students' advisors	Discuss with supervisors themselves	Observe resources accessibilities	Examine their contribution to your project

According to table one, research students may comprehend the role of their supervisors by observing their leadership style and examining their contribution to their projects. They can also acquire information from the student's academic advisors or read the university webpage and supervision handbook about supervisors' and students' roles and responsibilities. Sometimes, the supervision handbook can save the purpose, where the student and supervisors may discuss and clarify their responsibilities accordingly. In most cases, students may identify the availability and accessibility of resources and converse with their supervisors to comprehend their duties while describing the utilization of resources and cooperation strategies.

5.1.2 Contextual Focuses are Essential

Although some teachers' responsibilities call for changes, students must accept the contextual agreed practice until further notice. For example, students from a particular society may find it disturbing to be passive in the current learning environment because teachers apply dominance and authoritative supervision leadership. The role of teachers may be directing and controlling different from students' previous learning practices. While working for the change, the students must adjust to the situation and communicate their expectations harmoniously.

Most of the time, changes result from the appropriate and purposive conduct of those who demand it. Indeed, rioting and aggressive measures against teachers or institutions cannot save the purpose. Certainly, sometimes, teachers' supervision style may be the opposite of the student's expectations, and for students' voices to capture attention depend on their behavior. So, students should not expect change overnight or by violence, but good communication and patience may speed up the necessary changes. For example, a student who thinks the supervisors' roles differ from his expectations may call for a meeting to discuss the issue with the supervisors or appropriate personnel. In the meeting, he may describe his thought and expectations and propose the change accordingly. I believe that by doing so, the student suggestions may reach the mind of decision-makers, and changes may come more speedily than spreading rumors along the institution's corridors.

However, students should not be encouraged to abide by a practice that leads to their disability in learning. For instance, if the supervisors are not committed to students learning, students should not be silenced for that simply because it is the tradition in the learning context. Rather, students must speak their minds on the degree they are satisfied with their learning because it is the service they pay for. Education is a business like any other, and the customers, who are students, should inform their opinions that support bringing constructive changes to the higher education system.

On the other hand, they should not avoid or be discouraged from discussing issues that require changes. History has shown that research students have initiated many constructive changes and practices we observe in higher education today worldwide. For example, students' contributions have changed how supervisors communicate with students in supervision in some universities. A friend told me how students often reported lazy supervisors to the institution's management in his region, causing them to lose their positions. The management trusted students to evaluate teachers and acted when students performed the task. It needs students to eradicate irresponsible supervisors because they are the ones who understand their practices. If heard, students' voices can alter supervisors' practices and even the availability and accessibility of other resources. For instance, some students, such as doctoral and master's, are knowledgeable enough to assist others in the lower levels. Their involvement in helping others increases resources, and if encouraged, the institution with such students may benefit greatly.

Furthermore, if trusted, students may change different practices associated with fieldwork, tuition fees, and assessment. Sometimes, students encounter hardship in data collection based on their ethnicity or color that could not be there if institutional management cooperates with the community. Most institutions depend on communities for their studies, and community problems are the projects of institutions. So, one needs to educate community members, mostly informers, to research students, to understand the purpose and significance of students' studies. The information can help them cooperate with students regardless of ethnicity or other backgrounds. The primary issue is to educate the community to be aware of the higher education learning system, the reason behind students' investigations, and the functionality of the existing practices. If students' efforts in bringing changes in higher education obtain support, many problems could get solutions, and learning could be more meaningful and successful.

Many areas in research training require critics, and students are a vital tool for change. They are also essential stakeholders to seriously listen to in case of changes in teachers' roles, learning processes, and assessments. For example, sometimes, students desire to modify supervision practices for better cooperation and meet their expectations. However, they cannot do that without negotiation and agreement with institution management and supervisors based on the current methods. These two alliances are intense and sometimes isolated from students' expectations, and they may fail to comprehend their mistakes due to their loyalty. That is why it is essential to create an organ that stands on its own to safeguard the rights, suggestions, and views of institutions, supervisors, and students. The existence of an independent organ can bring liberty and freedom that stimulate students' creativity and facilitate changes in higher education. The more students comprehend their teachers' contextual practices, the more satisfied they become.

5.1.3 Students Dissatisfaction

In many universities, students do not receive the service they pay for or expect. Some expect more than the institution's provisions, and others have difficulty comprehending the information on universities' web pages. In most cases, students face challenges after enrolment, which create various setbacks. For example, most universities write positive, encouraging words and demonstrate accessibility of good services in their institutions, but students do not receive such services after enrollment. Sometimes, students are neglected and abandoned without supervisors months after enrolment, while universities claim to have adequate and caring teachers. Such a contradicting situation reduces students' motivation, and they may question the quality of their teachers. Likewise, students' lack of supervisors from the beginning of their enrolment may be one of the reasons for delay or dropout.

In other cases, students' dissatisfaction may bring a dilemma that institutions officials fail to organize human resources. It can raise the question of why the institution management admits students without knowing the state of their teachers. I believe this is one of the many practices that need changes in higher education such that students will enroll only when the supervisors are already available and accessible to them. As mentioned, students may observe several issues that need changes, but if their voices do not come to the decision-makers, their efforts will be unsuccessful.

Indeed, students need to identify the appropriate people or organs to communicate their challenges. Unfortunately, even when some universities describe the procedures to follow in solving disputes with supervisors, most students are still uncomfortable sharing their challenges with people who cannot be fair. Most so-called problem solvers in higher education are supervisors' colleagues, leaders, or employers. None of the three is neutral and can demonstrate proper judgment between the students and supervisors.

However, they are connected and familiar with each other, while the students are visitors who are short lasting.

Objective judgment from these three alliances (supervisors, leaders, and employers) can be challenging. Besides, most universities have no independent department dealing with supervision dispute cases. I have consulted many officials in different universities, and they confirmed that there is no such thing as a monitoring unit for supervisors in higher education. Instead, research students receive what they get from their supervisors, and when they experience dissatisfaction, they consult advisors, leaders, or supervisors' employers, who often dismiss the case. Therefore, in most cases, the supervisors have the autonomy to conduct supervision that suits them without anyone overseeing their practices or inspecting their strategies and performances. Thus, without external monitoring and evaluation, the institutional management (planners, implementers, and evaluators) can hardly evaluate their practices objectively.

Regrettably, when students complain about their teachers' conduct, they receive little attention from institutional actors. Some officials regard students who complain as stubborn, hypocrites, and unwilling to cooperate with their teachers. Students' backgrounds can be described as an obstacle to not understanding their teachers' roles and responsibilities. Yes, most students do not know the rules of the supervision game, and they sometimes desire supervisors to do their work. The lack of knowledge is the essence of this book to support research students to comprehend contextual teachers' duties.

Students' ignorance can be the source of their dissatisfaction and lack of support required. For instance, one of the informants, a Ph.D. student, complained that his supervisors did not inform him of the missed international conference. He was furious, saying the supervisors did not care about his interest. However, the information and procedures to follow to participate were on the department and the institution's webpage. Indeed, the student's statements indicated that he was unaware of his responsibility. He was the one who did not comprehend the situation correctly, not otherwise.

Indeed, the reputation of students who complain about their supervisors decreases if students complain irresponsibly. However, for genuine complaints, one should support students in finding a solution and succeed in their learning. Students sometimes have a dilemma reporting what they encounter in supervision because they do not know their roles and responsibilities. The situation widens the distance between the partners and increases their dissatisfaction. In the next chapter, we read about a doctoral student's dissatisfaction with the supervisors' pedagogical approach and how the so-called problem solver handled the case. The case is one of many supervision episodes students encounter in higher education, calling for an independent inspection unit for research student supervision.

Chapter 6

6.1 A Doctoral Student Experience

I mentioned earlier that this book's contents are partly stories of higher education stakeholders. One above all, I met a doctoral student who dropped from her studies recently with tears. She was frustrated and did not want to discuss it, although she allowed me to read her correspondence with the institution she dropped. The email from the doctoral student demonstrates her dissatisfaction with her supervisors' supervision pedagogy and that she was not expecting what she encountered.

The female doctoral student, Jackeline, was not catching up with her supervisors. She forwarded her concern to the postgraduate officers informing her experience with teachers and asking for help. The female doctoral student had had challenges coping with her supervisors' pedagogy for a long time, but she did not disclose it for reasons not in the email. Probably, she lacked the skills to communicate supervision challenges, or she did not understand the procedures required for such issues. Alternatively, as many students suppose, she did not believe she could obtain proper and adequate support.

Without a doubt, the email exchange between the student and the University official, with conversations with her and other students, motivated me to write about establishing a particular inspection unit in higher education. It has been challenging for institutional leaders, employers, and students to assess supervisors' work and effectiveness in students' learning worldwide. Moreover, some employers and institutional leaders are primarily supervisors' employers (especially privately owned institutions), and objectively monitoring supervisors' work can be difficult. Hence, students' voices about supervision weaknesses have become a crying of a fish in water, which goes unrecognized and unsupported.

So, this chapter will discuss the student's email and the responses she received from the person responsible for solving such problems. As I mentioned in the previous chapter, students in higher education have no one to advocate for them. Therefore, they hardly receive a fair judgment or solution when encountering a dispute with their supervisors. For example, let us consider the doctoral student's email complaining about supervision and the responses she received from the university official.

Please, read the email along the lines critically, putting yourself in the student's position, and think about how you could forward your complaints. Later take the role of the institutional official who claimed to attempt to solve the problem, and write in chapter ten how you could respond to the student's inquiry.

NOTE: I have obtained permission from the student and the university official to share the emails with my readers worldwide so long as they remain anonymous. I understand that the emails contain grammatical and writing errors, but they are understandable. I am exceedingly thankful for that.

The student email complaints read as follows.

"Dear Madam/Sir,

I have to say this to help other research students....

My supervisors ... comments on my progress and their pedagogy style are of concern. I started my Ph.D. studies in February ... I stayed almost three months without a supervisor, and I asked ... to supervise me. However, I was assigned ... as my principal supervisor.

These are among the comments I have been receiving in the course of supervision.

- *Undergraduates can do better than you.*
- *Master students understand better.*
- *your English is not good at all.*
- *your writing is not understood.*
- *your writing should be free from errors.*
- *your technical issues must be perfect (referencing and so on)*

This has happened on and on. We have discussed a little about the proposal. They [meaning the supervisors] asked me to write literature, I did it, arrange literature in different orders from paper and pencil to computer word, table, excel and so on. My supervisor... will say this, and the other one ... will say something else.

I took a breakthrough a long suspension, which ended on September 30. I decided to come back to focus on my proposal. I sent my work to my supervisors, but the references were not well structured due to errors that needed to be corrected in the RefWorks. My proposal was rewritten, something which appeared strange to me because I wanted to be taught how to do things, not how to copy from my supervisors' writing. Copying from my supervisor will not make me a good writer because their ideas look very artificial to my level and are not my ideas. Maybe if copying came after discussing my work together, that could be better understood. So, I took some of the rewritten ideas in my writing and not everything.

Unfortunately, after that, I had a meeting with…because I wanted to plan my work before X-mas with the thinking of coming back home (where I am now) for health purposes. This is what the supervisor … told me in the meeting.

- *you do not follow the instruction.*
- *you think you know better than us.*
- *you will not make it at all.*
- *you cannot change to other supervisors this time either.*
- *you have wasted our time, which could better be used by other students.*

… is a director of Pedagogy and Curriculum School. As little as I understand, a teacher cannot, by any means, say the above expressions in bullet 2, 3 and 5 to his/her students. A teacher can think of these expressions but not say it directly to a student. I was surprised, out of words and grateful that she had such a senseless feeling to say that to me directly. I thank her because I did not know a person in her position could have such destructive communication. I accepted to be vulnerable, but I am asking the postgraduate office to make sure that no other student will experience this because it is bullying.

The surprising thing is that people who bully do not think they do that because, after this conversation the supervisor … hugged me and wrote positively to the other supervisor… about our meeting and she did not think or write the bullying part of it. This is a call for the postgraduate office to do something to protect students from not experiencing such kind of bullying from their supervisors.

The total months I have been supervised from last year to this year are almost seven if we exclude those months I stayed without a supervisor. In my view, within this supervision time, I have accomplished a lot, although I have not submitted the required proposal. The materials I have accomplished could take me smoothly through writing chapters 1 to three of the dissertation and even in the discussion chapter. I was not expecting anyone to compare me with any other students but to take me as an individual.

My learning environment and experiences have been of many obstacles and contaminated with negative energy, which I am not used to. Therefore, I must end my studies if there is no better alternative from your side.

For the information, after my return from the suspension, I had an academic meeting with ...one time. I have not met with ... however, we have exchanged writing work.
I have paid some tuition fees, and I wonder whether I may get the money back.
With Regards,"

(I omitted the name of the student)

The email contains many valuable details that can help us understand the need for an inspection unit in higher education. However, I cannot discuss everything in this chapter and book because of the time limitation. Instead, I have discussed the same email demonstrating the student's weaknesses in supervision in the book "The skills required of students to effectively collaborate with academic supervisors" and "Articulating research students' expectations of a competent supervisor." These two mentioned books discuss the student's email, the shortfalls in supervision, and how to avoid them. In addition, I want to focus on prejudice in higher education in dealing with disputes between research students and supervisors in this book. The bias, misunderstandings, and subjectivity are the signs of the need for universities to establish a supervision unit to deal with such cases.

If we refer to the email, we may agree that the female student was looking for a change in supervision by saying, *"I have to say this to help other research students."* The statement indicates that she was thinking of others and looking forward to seeing support. The female student explained her dissatisfaction with the supervisors' pedagogy style and destructive comments on her progress. She also expressed disappointment with the last supervision meeting with the core supervisor. The female student desired to observe better communication between students and their supervisors rather than to be satisfied with the interaction she experienced. She lamented,

"I am asking the postgraduate office to make sure that no other student will experience this because it is bullying."

She categorizes her supervisor's conversation as a bullying experience, and the supervisors discourage her by mentioning several issues, including a waste of time that other students could better utilize. The difficulties of changing supervisors and the rebellious habit of the student by not following supervisors' instructions. In addition, the student could not cope with the supervisors' contradictory pedagogy style, where one directed her differently from the other. The doctoral student also mentioned the last meeting as the most challenging one, with a direct insult (according to her perspective) from the supervisor.

- *"you think you know better than us.*
- *you will not make it at all.*
- *you have wasted our time, which could better be used by other students."*

Many elements in the student's email indicate tiredness and screaming for help and change. In addition, the student's email informs of a break or suspension she had as a strategy to escape from her supervisors, but it did not solve the problem.

"I took a break through a long suspension, which ended on September 30...."

The break did not help much because she experienced similar challenges on her return. The main reason for her returning to the challenges is that she did not communicate her disputes, and a break could not silence or solve the problem but postponed it. She cried for help, but finally, it ended in the hand of the wrong person who could not comprehend the student's situation or solve the problem.

The student's complaint is a typical situation research students encounter in their learning contexts. Most of the time, students in higher education may need help, but they do not have reliable people to support them genuinely. As a result, some feel hopeless and work with unfunctional supervisors who cannot comprehend their needs and expectations for a long time. One reason for hopelessness is that students lack the support from university officials to solve their challenges. They do not have people to listen to their explanations for comfort and appropriate guidance. Even though the literature indicates most cases of student attrition emanate from failed supervision, little consideration has been directed to the supervision problems.

Likewise, those who receive and deal with students' complaints, challenges, and uncertainties are not skilled in solving them. Instead, they tend to lean on one side in their judgment because they deal with colleagues. In addition, it is unclear who is responsible for supporting students when they have a dispute with their supervisors. Sometimes, students must shout randomly to draw the attention of whoever can hear their voices and meet their needs.

In this case, Jackeline thought her complaint could bring better supervision to herself and others. Indeed, she might have heard or read about the challenges most research students encounter in supervision, which is why she mentioned helping others. However, she was unaware of the procedures to follow in solving supervision disputes and to whom she should address the matter. The responses indicate that students sent her complaints to the wrong channel because the head of school was the appropriate person.

6.1.1 The Head of School's Responses

Although the student expected to obtain help from the post-graduate officers, the department head or the school head responded to the student's inquiry. She received the following email demonstrating the head of the school's reaction. First, read the head of the department/school's response.

"Dear Student (I omit the name).

Your email has been referred to me as I am the head of school of your main supervisor, and therefore the school you are part of. I am very concerned to read your email as you raise several points about the progress of your PhD and your supervisors' behaviours and responsibilities.

Before I discuss your situation with you, and then your supervisors to get their perspective, I understand that you are an international student who began your Ph.D. with us last year. You experienced some health problems and so suspended your studies for some months. You have returned to ... (I omit the name of the University) *now, and your provisional year review is due, but you do not have a proposal that your supervisors feel is ready to be submitted to reviewers. You are finding the critical feedback on your work difficult to read/hear and feel that your supervisors' behaviour in your meetings has been unhelpful. I understand this is a stressful experience for you and am keen to work out what the problems are that we need to address. Do you have examples of your written work with feedback from your supervisors that you could send me? Do you have any audio recordings of supervision meetings that would elaborate on and support your comments below? Do you have a current draft proposal you could send me for me to ascertain whether a third opinion would help resolve some of the situations you are now in? Your concerns do not align with my experience of the professionalism of the supervisors as I know them, but perhaps something untoward has occurred.*

I am also concerned, however, as it appears that you have returned to your home country because you indicate that your health is still not fully improved. So, you were only back for two months? You are no longer in ...? (I omit the name of the University) *It is unacceptable for...* (I omit the name of the University) *international doctoral students to be absent without informing us and gaining the approval of the School of Graduate Studies. Your options are (a) to return to complete your PYR, (b) apply for a further suspension if you have a medical certificate to support your absence, or (c) apply to terminate your enrolment at The University of ... If your health is as poor as you imply and the relationship with your supervisors has broken down as you describe, I suspect that the last option might be best, and you indicate that you are considering ending your studies too in your email.*

However, I am keen to talk to you about this situation too, so can you please let me know where you are so I can work out the time difference and connect with you by Zoom to talk in the next week. Warm wishes,"

(I omitted the name of the head)

You read correctly. Yes, that is the response the student obtained for her complaints. It is the best way the head of the department thought could help the situation. Reading along the lines, one may realize that the head of the school/department had difficulty trusting the student and her complaint. The students did not complain about a criminal act, but unacceptable supervisors' pedagogy strategies, but the head of the school did not believe her. She stated, *"Your concerns do not align with my experience of the professionalism of the supervisors as I know them, but ...."*

Yes, the head of the school indeed knew the supervisors, they were her colleagues, and they shared the same employer. It is a strong statement for a student who informs of her experiences with the supervisors. It demonstrates that the student may be fabricated the issue or had a hidden agenda with the supervisors. Indeed, the department head may have a different experience with the teachers, but that should not interfere with or disqualify the students' experience initially before both partners convey their version.

So, the department head's email conveyed a statement that discouraged the student from further conversation. It is like saying to the student, "You are a big liar; my subordinates are not like that, they are professionals who are good supervisors, and they cannot act as you describe. They have a high reputation, and significantly to this department; we depend on them to function. So, NO, NO, NO, do not touch them; better pack your belongings and go than criticize people we regard highly.

On the other hand, the head of the school email indicates the dilemma she had in this case. But conversely, she demonstrated her willingness and intention to deal with the issue through the questions she asked. She also explained her purpose of collecting data on the case for further investigation. Read her statements.

"Do you have examples of your written work with feedback from your supervisors that you could send me? Do you have any audio recordings of supervision meetings that would elaborate on and support your comments below? Do you have a current draft proposal you could send me for me to ascertain whether a third opinion would help resolve some of the situations you are now in?

However, before asking such questions, the head could not remember the issue; she failed to comprehend the problem the student was talking about and asked her.

. ... what the problems are that we need to address.

She had a tough time dealing with the case, and it is like she was looking for a way to escape dealing with it altogether. It could be much better if she did not deal with the case because she was not the right person to deal with it. Indeed, the case raised confusion, and the school head was unaware of what to do and how to communicate the complaint appropriately. A case like this needs an independent agency with nothing to do with students' or supervisors' daily functionality. It should not be the task of someone who is not a supervisor's friend or colleague, nor the one affiliated with the department.

It was hard, but finally, the head of the department encouraged the student to withdraw from the studies to eliminate the case by the statement,

"(c) apply to terminate your enrolment at The University of ... If your health is as poor as you imply and the relationship with your supervisors has broken down as you describe, I suspect that last option [option c] *might be best...."*

The head of the school response represents the reactions most research students often receive from people responsible for resolving disputes between supervision partners. However, they face challenges caused by collegiality between the leaders and teachers; hence no one advocates for students.

The student, Jackeline, cried for help and expected to receive support, but simultaneously, she was unsure of the relevant persons or units to send the complaint to. Although she might think postgraduate officials could help, it was probably not the appropriate unit. She did not address the email to the department head, but it was forwarded to her, meaning maybe the head was the right person for such issues. Alternatively, the head might be the person to deal with all challenges in her department, including supervision issues. It was unclear, but one can argue that the department head obtained the assignment to deal with the case. Several speculations may arise, but one thing for sure is that the University in question had no independent supervision unit to deal with such matters.

Undeniably, the email shows the challenges most students encounter even when they have genuine complaints about their teachers. First, most are unaware of the organ or people responsible for supporting them or receiving complaints. Second, even when some universities inform students how to complain, students are skeptical of fair judgment. Usually, students are downgraded when pointing out the weaknesses of their teachers partly because of the diverse beliefs people still have about teachers' goddesses. Third, some institutions and cultures still demonstrate that teachers are life-givers, and their practices are unchallenged.

Fourth, some institutional and departmental leaders are themselves teachers' employers or colleagues and find a dilemma to question their approaches to students objectively. Fifty, most university leaders believe students are like tourists coming and going, so they protect the teachers. Finally, universities depend on teachers for policy implementations and student learning which are the foundation of all tertiary education businesses. So, the institutions' leadership and management need teachers; for these reasons, they protect them even though they cannot operate without students.

Let me put it in a figure to make it easy to remember these six aspects that deprive students of the right to be heard when they complain about supervisors' practices. Assume the girl in the figure is a university student who should familiarize herself with the institutional concepts and take advantage of her teachers in learning. However, if she is unfamiliar with the supervision game's rules, the system can be deaf to her interests, needs, and expectations even when she shouts loudly; the three concepts dominate decisions.

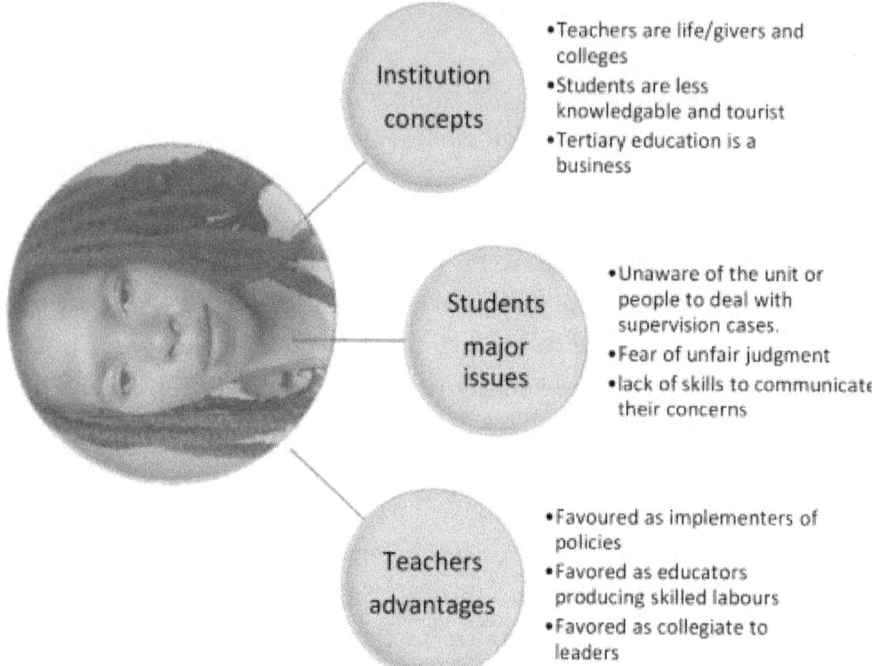

Figure 9. Reasons for Deafness in Students' Complaints

According to Figure nine, the student's voice is hindered by nine principal factors from three significant aspects, thus, aspects within the students, the institution, and the teachers. First, teachers' central concept as life-givers and students less knowledgeable on the procedures and rules of supervision games bring bias in finding a resolution to supervision disputes. In addition, most institutional management and leadership believe education is a business and teachers play central roles. Second, the student may be unaware of who deals with their concerns and where to send their inquiry. So, the majority may keep silent, especially those lacking communication skills, and may be discouraged if there is unfair treatment or judgment. On the other hand, teachers are favored by institutional leadership and management due to their collegiality, roles as policy implementers, and the producers of skilled laborers.

Again, research students face the challenge of being trusted by higher education actors in their complaints, discouraging them from communicating their concerns altogether. So, the current supervision system makes students who inform their experiences in supervision think twice about the consequences. For instance, in the case of Jackeline, the graduate officers forwarded her claim to the head of the school to deal with it, possibly intending to solve it. However, the head imposed the judgment without further discussion with the partners involved, motivating the student to withdraw.

If we refer to the concept of "teachers as life-givers," we agree that some institutions continue with such a philosophy leaving them uncriticized. So often, no one openly conveys or corrects the weaknesses of tertiary education teachers because of the life-givers perspectives. They give life to the institution, the students, and society. So, instead, the leadership works hard to cover teachers' mistakes and avoid offending them because they have such a concept in mind. So, as we know, actions converse louder than words, and thus, when complications enter the supervision arena, the leadership judgment demonstrates teachers' positions openly as uncriticized life-givers.

For example, if we refer to the emails, the school's (department) head did not comprehend that teachers' pedagogy could bother the student, so she defended the supervisors. She wondered what the student complained about and wanted her to pack and leave the institution and teachers alone. However, the supervisors might have effectively supervised other students, and their supervision methods worked well for others but not for Jackeline. Therefore, the student needed someone to listen and comprehend her situation objectively before coming up with a biased conclusion.

Unfortunately, in most cases, supervisors do not always supervise students in the same pair. The supervisors may supervise different students with different partners or colleagues. For example, Jackeline's supervisors had no other students they supervised together but other colleagues, hence new partners. Typically, supervisors supervise different students from various departments with other colleagues. Even the department head was not a leader for both the supervisors in the case of Jackeline's issue, but the leader of the core supervisor. In the student's email, she called her core supervisor, the director, "... *is a director of Pedagogy and Curriculum School.*" It means that in the department, there were different disciplines and specializations. It will not be mistaken to predict that the other supervisor came from another department and had his head and maybe supervised other students with other supervisors.

Therefore, there is interchangeability and interconnections of supervisors and students from different departments and disciplines. Moreover, as mentioned earlier, most universities encourage interdisciplinary interconnections and a learning nature for integrating academics and students. The system works well for those who comprehend their roles and responsibilities. Most universities attempt to avoid extreme specialization, covering up inadequate human resources, widening knowledge, and creating flexibility for graduates in the job market.

6.1.2 Walk Away as a Strategy

Indeed, the head of the school knew how difficult it was to be objective; that is why she encouraged the students to walk away. Dealing with supervision disputes needs expertise that most leaders lack and no organ to provide them with qualifications in the current practices. For example, the head of the school was in a dilemma, and her email demonstrates two issues. The first is her willingness to deal with the case, and the second is her judgemental discouragement. She is not alone because most higher education leaders find a predicament when dealing with teachers' and students' supervision challenges or conflicts. They know they cannot be fair to students because teachers are their colleagues; they need and are familiar with them.

Consequently, the best way to avoid biases, confusion, and discouragement is for leaders to encourage students to walk away. Unfortunately, institutional and departmental leaders may not be fair and appropriate persons to deal with disputes between students and supervisors. Most leaders avoid dealing with such controversial cases by asking students to walk away. In most cases, the leaders attempted to demonstrate the challenges associated with becoming judges for such cases. Disputes in supervision need exceptional listeners with supervision experiences, especially those without direct connections with teachers and students. Teachers' colleagues should not deal with such cases because they can hardly be objective. Most of the time, the students are the ones to be rebuked and discouraged from forwarding their complaints and possibly forced to walk away.

We can see that the head applied the same strategy of eliminating the complaints and being safe with her cabin crew without considering the student's situation. The main aim of the school head in choosing the option "©" was to end the ambiguity, conflict, and complaints. Unfortunately, even when the department head indicated the willingness to solve the problem, the rest of the email's content could not back up that intention. For instance, she contends, *"... I am keen to talk to you about this situation ..."* Really!! Contradicted the statement, *"Your concerns do not align with my experience of the professionalism of the supervisors as I know them."* It might be challenging to ask for an extended conversation after such a substantial judgment.

The student might have thought that if the school's leader rejected her complaint while she knew little about the case, how could she be fair? It did not make sense for someone representing the student and supervisors to lean on one side like that before receiving all the required data. But, at the same time, the head was sincere, saying that she knew the supervisors; it was a confirmation that she knew them, and that is where the difficulty lies. It is hard for institution leaders to be objective with people they know over those regarded as visitors.

Without further consideration, the head of the school had no idea or did not care how her responses affected the student from opening for more details. She openly demonstrated a strike against the student's allegations and gave her a red card by asking her to walk away. It also indicated the head's failure to propose a better alternative, in which the student wrote by writing, *"... I must end my studies if there is no better alternative from your side."* Thus, the student had not decided to end her studies but was undecided and awaited a helping hand. If you re-read the student's email, you may realize she wanted someone to challenge her decision to end her studies with a better solution.

For example, she could be grateful to obtain support to reunite her with the same supervisors with new pedagogical strategies or someone who could support her work with new supervisors with better approaches. Finally, she mentioned changing supervisors, indicating that the game was not over for her; she wanted to continue her studies.

The head could influence the student's decision and change the discontinuity perspective, but it seemed she was for the teachers. She claimed she was keen to support and ask genuine questions in the email, but she disavowed the support by indicating the alternative © of walking away as the best for the student.

The head did not even think the teacher could have bad days, which could cause problems in supervision sessions. She did not believe the diverging perspectives on the roles and responsibilities of teachers and students could create misunderstandings about the quality of teachers. Likewise, the diverging academic backgrounds of the supervisors could lead to providing divergence instructions to the student; instead, she rejected the claim and content that,

"Your concerns do not align with my experience of the professionalism of the supervisors as I know them...."

Indeed, her statement is a typical example of how teachers' seniority can affect students' learning.

As a result, the student's case reached nowhere, and her wish to continue her studies and change supervision practice was in vain. It shows that students' subordination in the formal education system and higher education has been the norm and has created deafness to solve many supervision problems. Most universities suffer student attrition, yet practitioners and leaders do not value students. The head of the department's statement indicates how valueless the student was for the department, institution, and society. If the student was resourceful, the head of the department could not afford to lose her, but she ignored her and indicated her worthless.

Moreover, the department head demonstrates the habit of her crew members. It means that teachers in her department do not care much about students' demands or trust them. She reflects this character through her statement of unbelief and encourages the student to walk away. In this case, the student was called a liar, a fabricator, sick and stressed individual who intends to destroy the supervisor's reputation; hence she should walk away.

6.1.3 Predicaments Dealing with Complaints

In the previous chapters, I provided people's historical perceptions about teachers' roles, responsibilities, and positions. The information mentioned above prepared you to understand why the head of the school might have responded in that defensive way. However, it could not be straightforward to comprehend the head of the department's responses if I did not discuss teachers' historical positions and roles in different societies. The diversity in teachers' duties depends on the accessibility of learning resources, the societal norms on teachers' position as life/givers, and the hierarchical culture between learners and teachers. Therefore, referring to the previous chapter on teachers' positions, you can comprehend why the head protected the supervisors before listening to the student. Nevertheless, her habit may give readers insight into why an independent organ should scrutinize teachers' practices.

I will not discuss the email content intensely in this section. Still, at least you have obtained a glimpse of an example of the challenges research students encounter and how the head of schools or leaders deal with supervision cases. Of course, if the head became fair, the only thing that could happen is to ask the student to change the supervisor. But, on the other hand, in some cases, if the student is allowed to turn to other supervisors and ends up with other problems, the result could be withdrawal. Therefore, in many cases, the students are the losers when they encounter challenges with supervisors; thus, they lose by being asked to change supervisors or their degrees if the new supervisors do not meet their expectations.

In an extended conversation, it showed that the student, in this case, withdrew from her studies. Thus, although I cannot judge the case and think she was a victim, she encounters challenges that had solutions if the institution had an independent unit with qualified educators who could handle supervision cases dealt with it. For example, the head mentioned the rules concerning international students, which the student had already broken by leaving the institution without permission. Indeed, several issues went wrong in this supervision. Even the head could be overwhelmed dealing with such a complicated case on top of her teaching, supervising research students, and leadership duties.

From another perspective, contrary to withdrawing, the student could take different steps to obtain the desired service, but she lacked some vital skills. One can read the books I recommended earlier to comprehend the actions the students could have taken and the skills that could facilitate her cooperation with supervisors. The books may inform the qualities supervisors expect from students and how students should acquire the vital abilities to combat diverse challenges.

All in all, now you may read both emails and ask how they could better handle the situation. It may help if you read the emails repeatedly while examining the message and the fairness of the suggestions the head of the school wrote. You may come to the point where you think of having an independent unit to deal with supervision issues in each university.

Most students I conversed with suggested that the head of schools or departments should deal with academic issues related to teaching and learning, ensuring physical and human resources, and delegating duties. Of course, they could also be responsible for the teaching and examinations, but someone else who can act neutrally could be accountable when a conflict arises in supervision. For example, some research students commented that people sitting around the same table for lunch while sharing their social and private lives sometimes fail to discipline each other.

Therefore, my primary objective is to encourage higher education decision-makers to formulate a policy to establish a supervision unit for research students. As indicated, the department would deal with supervision issues, including difficulties. The unit will have different sections, including the dispute section, to deal with challenges in cooperation between students and supervisors, supervisors and peers, and even institutional leaders and supervisors.

However, before concluding the wish for an independent unit for supervision cases in higher education, we should comprehend the current process. Therefore, let us look at higher supervision and student attrition.

Chapter 7

7.1 Student Attrition Statistics

The most challenging problem in higher education today is student attrition. Diverse findings demonstrate the seriousness and scope of the situation, which is partly associated with a failure in supervision. In addition, the scholarly literature has shown that institutions are affected by student attrition problems differently, with thousands of causes. Indeed, student attrition affects all higher education stakeholders in one way or another, but students are the most affected (Urassa, 2021). Even though researchers have indicated possible measures to reduce student attrition in higher education, the problem persists. If you read publications by Beer & Lawson (2018), Maher & Macallister (2013), O'Keeffe (2013), and others of the kind, you may comprehend the scope of the challenge and the proposal provided by them.

The scholar's central concept emphasized students' good relationships with their supervisors. Currently, most students and supervisors lack skills that facilitate cooperation leading to unfunctional relations. For example, Grant (2005, 2008) explained the dilemma students face in their relationship with supervisors, which sometimes resembles an enslaved person and master. Likewise, scholars mentioned students' lack of belonging to the institution and the learning community as another reason for withdrawing. Indeed, many students, especially doctoral students in humanity (education and art), undertake research project individually in most universities, which make them isolated and have no relevant network. The detachment from the institutional communities (departments, sections, and society) for these students may lead to problems that may end in students withdrawing. Although the sense of belonging is vital, scholars demonstrated that most students risk dropping out due to lacking connection. In most cases, students must connect with supervisors who should introduce them to other networks.

Undeniably, one may argue that supervisors' inability to introduce students to the learning environment and support them in building relevant, productive networks has failed many students. Indeed, the support to integrate into the learning community is for international students, locals, and all students. A good supervisor cares for students' well-being and comfort in their learning environment, knowing that students cannot concentrate and focus on their studies without being part of others. Nevertheless, unfortunately, most supervisors do not look after their student's sense of belonging, and some have no idea of their students' networking problems. As a result, many students stay isolated, which causes a challenge to focus on their studies, ending in withdrawal.

Unfortunately, student attrition is a challenge that has affected many higher education stakeholders. Scholars have confirmed the dilemma by highlighting its magnitude and calling it different names. For example, some have perceived student attrition as "a wicked problem" (Beer & Lawson, 2018) and a scandal (Gardner, 2009). Likewise, Fisher & Engemann (2000) have baptized student attrition as the most persistent and problematic issue in the history of higher education. So, wicked, scandal, and the most persisting challenge are among the many names that indicate the seriousness of the problem and the unpleasant experience it provides to society. It is a sign that the problem is now known and that higher education stakeholders should not just talk about it but take measures and find sustainable solutions.

At the same time, student attrition does not respect the continent, country, or institution; instead, it is a global challenge. According to Maher and Macallister (2013), in Australia, the Department of Education and Training, back in 2004, reported undergraduate attrition rates of 21.2% and 18.0% for domestic and international students, respectively. Gabb, Milne, and Cao (2006) wrote about attrition in one of the universities in Australia from 1994-2003 to be at 25%. Similarly, O'Keeffe's (2013) study showed that higher education student attrition rates reached 20% in Australian universities. In Canada, Fisher and Engemann (2009) reported 43% of student attrition in Ontario's colleges between 1998-2003. Whirls in the Netherlands, Meeuwisse, Severiens, and Born (2010) informed HE student withdrawal rate was 20% to 10% for vocational and university education, respectively.

Likewise, a similar problem has reached other parts of the world. For instance, student attrition is challenging in many institutions in the USA. Indeed, Fisher and Engemann (2009) stated that North America's student dropout rate in higher education was 30-40%. Similarly, Golde (2000, 2005) argued that at least 40% of Ph.D. students withdraw from their studies in America. He also indicated some studies that estimated the attrition of doctoral students to be between 40-50%, whereas the undergraduate attrition rate was 10-20% at selective institutions.

Similarly, Demetriou & Sciborski (2011) informed that student attrition in America has been terrifying for the last hundred years and that only 50% of those who join higher education complete their degree. In another study, Mayo, Helms, and Codjoe (2004) learned that the retention rate in the University System of Georgia in 2011 was 59.8%. Thus, the report on the challenges facing higher education in the US aligns with what other scholars informed, and one can generalize by saying the attrition is 50%.

On the other hand, Johnes & McNabb (2004) examined the UK situation and reported that student attrition is a persisting problem. For instance, the student attrition rate in HE raised from about 13-16% in the late 1970s and early 1980s to 19-25% in the 1990s. The scholars said student attrition might increase if no severe measures are taken to address the problem.

According to Higher Education Funding Council for England (HEFCE) (2005) annual report and accounts in the UK, 19 % of Ph.D. part-time students and 57% of full-time students complete their studies within five years. While 71% of full-time and 34% of part-time tend to complete their tasks within seven years. The information discloses two significant challenges in higher education in the UK; thus, students delay completing their degrees, and some drop out.

Equally, Johnston (2005) in Becker & Becker (2008) revealed that the University of Edinburgh, Leeds, London, Manchester, and Ulster had 22.0%, 8.6%, 11.0%, 8.6%, and 22.0% attrition rates, respectively, in the period 2003-2004. Likewise, Kettell (2020), when discussing young adult carers[4] applying the work of Sempik and Becker (2013, 2014), informed that 29% of the students dropped out. Thus, the attrition problem is higher education's global challenge and the primary reason associated with supervision.

In South Africa, Zulu & Mutereko (2020) acknowledge that student attrition is the main obstacle to success in higher education. Nevertheless, it seems the challenge persists and is increasing because, in 2011, Herman informed that 20% of doctoral students drop out before completing their studies. For her, the practice creates a feeling of loss, failure, waste, and guilt. Recently statistics indicated that universities in Africa have a student attrition rate of 50 %, despite their challenge in accessing higher education. For example, less than 15% of people desiring higher education degrees in South Africa have access. However, of those who join universities, 50% drop sometimes within the first year of their degree, and only 15 % complete their degrees timely (Bokana, 2010).

Scholars have also described some valuable suggestions to reduce student attrition. For instance, Beer and Lawson (2018) recommended that the wickedness of this challenge in HE requires attention from diverse sources and actors from learning institutions and beyond. In addition, the problem requires a solution that cares for students' academic and social well-being while facilitating their integration. The scholars reminded us that HE students must feel valued, be accepted, and have equal access to diverse learning supporting agencies and resources. They should also obtain support to become part of the learning community.

This book does not intend to provide mathematical details of each country and continent regarding student attrition. However, it demonstrates that student attrition is a severe challenge requiring attention from higher education stakeholders worldwide.

Indeed, most students are disappointed by supervisors in different ways, and their experiences kill their degrees. For example, if a research degree student withdraws due to isolation, I think it is the supervisor's weakness not to share networking strategies with the student. Again, if the student drops out due to academic and supervision issues is the supervisor's helplessness and failure in supervision. It indicates that the supervisor is not available, accessible, and approachable enough for the student to benefit from his network. Most weaknesses in overseeing where the supervisors fail to integrate the student into the learning community lead to isolation. Indeed, some students have dropped out because they could not cope with the learning culture, indicating supervisors' shortfalls in supporting students.

Thus, tertiary education and research students depend on their supervisors exceptionally for learning, enculturation, and general well-being. The more caring the supervisors are to students, the more students gain a state of belonging, and the better they learn the culture and integrate themselves into the learning community. Students who are included and integrated into the learning community reduce their supervisors' roles and responsibilities accordingly. Likewise, those less included and integrated may have challenges working with other agencies and depend on their supervisors for almost everything, increasing their duties.

Therefore, it is the supervisors' weaknesses when students drop out of their studies, if not the issues related to themselves, such as health, finance, and other personal factors. Of course, some students have dropped out due to emotional hindrances, but most of those who withdraw from supervision causes blame their supervisors for their failure. Often, for students with financial and academic capability, without personal issues, the primary cause of their dropout is associated with supervision. So, the student's decision to withdraw caused by supervisors' leadership indicates one or several matters are not functioning appropriately.

Consequently, it is the right time to think differently if the universities have been troubled by student attrition for a long time and have research findings demonstrating that student attrition is partly a failure in supervision. It may be helpful to consider surveillance untraditionally by introducing an independent unit for monitoring and evaluating the practices and guiding supervisors accordingly.

7.1.1 Handling Students' Complaints

As mentioned earlier, higher education institutions have no special department dealing with supervision matters. Some have established a postgraduate office to deal with diverse issues, including supervision, but lack experts. Other universities employ department leaders to allocate, change, and resolve supervision cases, but they are not objective in their decisions. For example, in the student case of the earlier email, the institution had no department special for supervision concerns, and the student thought postgraduate officers were the right persons to deal with such cases.

If they had a special department for supervision disputes, the student could not wait long to inform her challenges. She could have known the correct people to share the problem with and solve her dilemma. However, instead, she was frustrated and took a suspension to maybe think about the supervision situation and return to the University. So, the student suspended her studies rather than finding the right person to support her, and she had health issues mentioned in the emails that hindered her from focusing on the instructions properly.

Likewise, she had conversed with other students and thought they had a similar problem; otherwise, she could not write, *"I have to say this to help other research students...."*

Undoubtedly, the student had a dilemma that most higher education students encounter in understanding the correct department or people to deal with diverse supervision challenges. Despite most universities informing students that they can complain and change whatever they desire, the process tends to be complicated and discouraging. In addition, students do not receive adequate support to process their complaints or guidance on addressing their frustrations. Regrettably, as we have seen, some students' complaints reach nowhere in higher education systems, and sometimes students who report their disappointments receive the blame and are forced to walk away.

Indeed, many cases indicate a lack of support and guidance for students in higher education to deal with disputes under supervision. For instance, one student, Helen, informed me of the sexual harassment she encountered in supervision, where one of her supervisors often demanded to meet her at home. The supervisor scheduled supervision meetings at awkward hours, asking her to meet without negotiation. He always pretended he was to travel the day after for the international conference or other issues as reasons for the emergency meetings. As a result of the short notice, the student could not attend the meetings scheduled by the supervisor in question, which created confrontation and misunderstandings. The supervisor decided to destroy her reputation and manipulated the other supervisor, and as a result, they both neglected her.

Helen was an independent student, so when she was dealing with rewriting the research proposal at the beginning of her studies, she did not care much about the absence of her supervisors. However, as in many universities, research students cannot move to the next learning stage without supervisors' acknowledgment. So, she needed them to review her work and recommend its quality to move forward. So, supervisors did not respond to her invitation when she scheduled a meeting, even when she reminded them. Furthermore, she had a deadline to submit her proposal; therefore, she did it without the supervisors' acceptance.

Unfortunately, the proposal needed corrections, and the student wanted the supervisors' expert advice, but they sabotaged her. They did not respond to the scheduled meeting, and she decided to send her work to them, asking for their input and indicating where she desired their comments. Still, instead, she received additional harassing comments from the supervisor, which ended with, "*You do not know how to work with your supervisors, and you do not learn to be nice; learn to be a good girl.*" Helen believes that the reaction toward supervisors' practice disappointed the supervisor. She complained to one academic advisor about the sexual harassment she had been receiving and other comments from the core supervisor.

The advisor replied to Helen's inquiries, saying, "*Your core supervisor is the most respectable person we have ever had, and I am sure there must be something wrong you have done*

Wao!! She also asked to change to a female supervisor for her good. However, no one confronted the male supervisor who harassed her or sent him a warning letter; instead, the advisor dismissed the case. Yes!! What support from the advisor!! As a substitute, the advisor blamed the student for displaying her body instead of rebuking the teacher and supporting the student, who demanded appropriate service and respect in supervision.

Indeed, it might be a good idea to inform the students about proper dress, but advisors must not wait until a student reports a case of sexual harassment to do that. For example, if the dress code was necessary, the student could have received the cultural dressing rules information in the orientation programs. However, when a student reports supervisors' unacceptable conduct, there should not be an excuse from those dealing with such cases. Giving such an excuse can legitimate the supervisors' harassment habit and indicates unprofessionalism because even when students are completely naked, no one should legalize harassing them.

Sometimes students have been disqualified because they complained about their supervisors who have the institutions' and society's reputation. Supervisors with vital positions when they disappoint students, the institution leaders and managements desire to expel students. We must not forget that teachers are the constructors of knowledgeable and skilled individuals who obtain employment in universities and other places. Some advisors were the same supervisors' students; disciplining them can be a dilemma. For example, some advisors capture their jobs because of the recommendations from the same supervisors, and they cannot do anything to destroy their employment. Instead, students are the ones to carry the burden and ought to accept whatever practice they encounter under supervision.

Indeed, students who filed cases concerning supervisors' weaknesses are rarely listened to or believed by those dealing with such cases. Among other reasons for disbelief is that the students' complaints, as mentioned, are looked upon by supervisors' former students, colleagues, the persons they recommended as advisors or supervisors' employers. Therefore, when these people receive students' claims about the supervisors, they encourage them to drop out to eliminate the complaints.

The walk-away solution is what most students obtain, just as it was with the Jackeline. If we refer to the email, the head of the school argued that the student desired to drop out, but she could not rate it as the best option if she had an alternative. It indicates that the school head was glad the student came up with the standard solution (walk away). Indeed, although the student mentioned her plan to withdraw in the email, she also indicated her willingness to continue by inviting a better alternative. She asserted, "... *I must end my studies if there is no better alternative from your side.*" Indeed, there was no better alternative from the school head because that is the most desired one.

Generally, the student cried for help, as many do with different voices without being heard or supported. The doctoral student's incidence is typical of many experiences most higher education students encounter when they report their challenges in supervision. The student complained about the supervisor's pedagogical style and was encouraged to drop her studies. Her complaint was not a crime; the issue could be solved by asking supervisors to cooperate and establish similar priorities and expectations with the student.

Now, if a non-crime case ended with the student being encouraged to withdraw, what about those who report crimes such as sexual abuse, stealing students' projects, or supervisors' manipulation for financial benefits? I heard many supervision disputes between less knowledgeable (students) and more knowledgeable (supervisors), indicating taking advantage of students' ignorance. Again, students are at high risk of not having an independent supervision unit with officials to advocate for them. In most cases, the current supervision system does not care for students, and mostly, "NO ONE BELIEVES THEM."

We often hear from social media about abusive practices happening in higher education learning environments. Often, people explain what happened in their educational lives many years ago and cannot speak it out due to the fear of not being believed. For example, I read one story of an eighty-four-year-old woman explaining sexual harassment she experienced when she was twenty-seven at a university. She could not report the incident to the academic advisors because she knew the person could not believe her story. Besides, the teacher who harassed her was friendly to everybody, including the advisor. So, she kept silent, but the incident left her with trauma, and she could not marry and have children like other women. It was an unpleasant and unforgettable experience she repeatedly encountered in supervision. Unfortunately, the business of knowledge in exchange for sex was happening behind the supervision scene.

7.1.2 Fighting for Resources

Another issue that may bring a dispute in supervision is the ownership of research outcomes. Many students cry for their right to ownership of projects and the money generated or allocated to the research projects. Some students, as mentioned, introduce their supervisors to their projects. For example, some doctoral students may conduct research that becomes a big money-generating project. Still, supervisors may control the projects, and the student obtains only the degree and become no part of the projects after graduation. Unfortunately, such cases are many, especially in science disciplines, and sometimes students' voices are ignored, and their ownership rights cease. Students need independent experts; otherwise, their rights are taken before their faces. With no one to defend them, such cases usually end up on the desk of the head of the departments, where the judgments may, as usual, favor the teachers.

Indeed, some other people are affected by their experience in higher education for a lifelong, and it may be something that could be prevented by having an independent unit to deal with supervision cases. As mentioned, the few students communicating their encounters in the current system receive little or no support to win their cases. Most withdraw without forwarding their complaints, especially those without connection to the academic community because they know they will receive unfair results.

Moreover, the formal education system at all levels has a bureaucratic procedure that discourages many from complaining. Therefore, the students who desire their petitions to be solved immediately find it difficult to deal with the system. As a result, the cases may delay and prolonged for months without a conclusion or solution until the complainers give up.

Chapter 8

8.1 A Transformation Required

We have seen the advantage of experts examining teachers' work through school inspection policy, which many call school supervision today. The name has changed from inspection to supervision after the inspectors' expertise increased, allowing them to provide practical advice to teachers and other school stakeholders. We also observe different inspectors' tasks and evaluations and how they affect teachers' employment and promotion. However, the central mission of school inspectors or supervisors in primary and secondary schools is to assess and provide expert advice to teachers, heads of schools, and their employers or policymaker.

Contrary, supervision in tertiary education is exceptional and individual teaching. The teaching is complex, private, and has no specific structure or experts for monitoring and evaluation. Even though the publications by Greimel-Fuhrmann & Geyer (2003), Husbands & Fosh (1993), and Lee & Manathunga (2010) agreed that higher education supervision is teaching and guiding research students without overseeing the work of teachers.

Other scholars with a similar perspective on supervision as teaching are Saroyan & Amundsen (2001) and Spooren, Mortelmans & Denekens (2007) (to mention a few). The scholars who agree on supervision as teaching express their concern about its practices and support assessing the quality of teaching. They are apprehensive because if teachers performed their duties correctly and other factors constantly remained good, most higher education institutions could not suffer student attrition at such a high rate (refer to student attrition statistics).

Indeed, postsecondary education teachers are the major determinants of the successful learning process and the outcomes of research students. As mentioned earlier, the challenging relational supervision atmosphere can signify the lack of vital skills to the partners and has led to many challenges.

Undoubtedly, some students have withdrawn from their studies because, among others, of difficulties cooperating with supervisors. Regardless of students' motivation and resource accessibility, the supervision relation can be a stumbling block for students not attaining their learning goals. Typically, as we have discussed, when students fail to cooperate with their supervisors, they generally tend to change the supervisor or withdraw.

It may be the right time for higher education institutions to find sustainable solutions to students' supervision problems. In the sample case, we have also seen that the heads of departments responsible for finding solutions had a dilemma. Therefore, introducing an independent organ with experts to inspect the supervision process may be a sustainable solution. Indeed, teachers' problems with students cannot be listened to by their leaders or colleagues, nor solved by students' evaluation procedures applied by many universities today. It needs experts with a neutral position and autonomy in judging the case objectively. The head of departments or institutions may have a predicament to be impartial to students, especially when the complaints involve supervisors with known statuses in the institution and community. Therefore, experts from an independent department with knowledge about supervision challenges may be relevant to assessing the supervision process and dealing with the training of supervisors and dispute cases.

8.1.1 A Need for Autonomous Expertise

In the previous chapters and sections, I have discussed the favor supervisors receive due to the perception of being life-givers and knowledgeable. No wonder teachers acquire such good names due to their ability to eradicate ignorance and construct a workforce for societies. Regrettably, some misuse the trust by neglecting their duties and do not comprehend learners' needs and expectations. As a result, they abuse such confidence, demonstrate what pleases their employers, and maintain their positions.

However, all the cases in this book demonstrate the loyalty teachers obtain from their leaders and employers against learners. The mutual connection between teachers, institutional leaders, and owners is unbreakable, and such trust in teachers may influence the decisions they make regarding supervision cases. Furthermore, the confidence in teachers affects how the institutions treat families, who are the customers of educational services. Sometimes institutions may lose the trust of other stakeholders by holding on to dream killers teachers. For instance, one mother explained how a tertiary education teacher abused her daughter without consequences. Unfortunately, currently, people join higher education even before their twenties with little experience with the harsh learning environment. So, without guidance, they can quickly be trapped in the hands of dream killers and fail to handle the situation cleverly. Of course, I do not mean people below the twenties are not brilliant, but some have little life experience compared to elderly students. Moreover, some students are away from their shepherd (parents and guardians) for the first time, pursuing their first or second degree. Likewise, we know that when people are in their twenties, their outer beauty may attract many, including dream killers.

Let us turn to the mother I want to talk about; regrettably, the woman sent her daughter abroad for a second degree. The daughter, Diana, met with a sexual predator supervisor who consecutively misused her for almost six months.

First, the supervisor frightened her by saying that the learning environment was brutal and that males were dangerous. Then, the supervisor informed her that she could be safer if she allowed a male individual like him to protect her. Then, when the supervisor obtained her trust, he became the trouble he was talking about by abusing her, controlling, and damaging her psychologically.

Finally, the girl could not take it and had no courage to discuss the issue with her advisors. She decided to withdraw from her studies at the end of the sixth month of her master's degree. When she reached home, the girl explained her experience to her mother. The woman contacted the institution's management in vain, and because she did not obtain cooperation from the institutional officials, she informed the police. The police dealt with the case for months by asking questions to the institutional leadership and teachers, including the supervisor. Finally, they informed the mother of their investigation results, which ended in no evidence to charge the supervisor.

Although this case has much information, I do not want to discuss it in detail. Instead, I only inform what I have permission for; any other issues should remain to the incident's victims. Without a doubt, there are several unanswered questions in this case. For example, one could ask why the student did not report the incident to any institutional official early. It may disturb others to wonder why she did not talk to peers, establish a case, and expose the teacher while she was still enrolled. The other can respond by saying maybe she was not okay or she was among people who consider teachers as gods.

It may also indicate that people around her were not trustworthy, or she had non-to communicated with them during her six months stay except the predator. The student might be isolating herself or being separated to justify the danger of not having someone like the predator. Of course, no one can respond to these questions or speculations except the student. Indeed, if the university had a supervision unit known by students with experts having the autonomy to solve supervision cases fairly, Diana could have reported the case than withdrawn.

No, it is incorrect to keep silent, and it is not wise not to establish a department to oversee supervision in tertiary education. Honestly, it is unfair to let people who once were life-givers be life-destroyers on our faces. When a research degree student withdraws from the studies because of any cause, including supervision challenges, it is the death of a degree. The failure of supervisors is also of the institution which enrolled the student and provided hope that it could fulfill his needs and expectations. If students do not attain their learning goals due to weaknesses in supervision, it is the institution's failure. Therefore, it is time for universities to fulfill learners' expectations by establishing an independent organ to monitor supervision practices. The department could also provide expert advice and deliver fair resolutions in disputes between the supervision partners.

Although I have pointed out students' challenges in supervision, I do not mean supervisors are not facing problems. I discussed the challenges supervisors might face in supervising students due to the multicultural and interdisciplinary nature of current tertiary education learning. Besides, students have diverse perspectives and behave differently based on their learning intentions. For example, some supervisors must deal with "Luciferic students," cultural issues, employment conditionalities, and other factors. However, the book does not focus on supervisors' challenges and expectations but purposively advocates for students without apologizing.

Indeed, academics have widely written about the challenges they face in supervision. They have mentioned the increased diversity and student population as among the challenges. So, now is the time for students to air their voices and make their situations and suggestions known. Most research students I conversed with have had challenges that institutional officials could not solve because of the same dilemmas (collegiality and bias) described earlier. Therefore, the demand for universities to establish an independent organ with experts to monitor the supervision process is valid. The professionals will support supervisors and students with knowledge and solve diverse issues to eliminate supervision challenges.

Some universities have introduced supervision programs and courses attempting to support supervisors. However, such programs are conducted by people who sometimes have no experience supervising research students. They are just imagining and sometimes have no idea of the effect of their message in supervision. Thus, it is not strange to see people with bachelor's degrees becoming experts telling professors how to supervise research students they have never supervised. No wonder some experienced university teachers do not attend such supervision programs conducted with inexperienced advisors because sometimes they provide elusive information. At the same time, the advisors cannot handle supervision disputes objectively when they land on their desks.

Indeed, some academics become disappointed by those philosophizing academic supervision as technical performance. In most cases, some advisors discuss the supervision of students as a duty requiring a formula applicable to all students. They emphasize timely completion to all students as if they have the same learning needs and abilities. However, supervision is not a mechanical act but a relational one that needs care, as in all other human relationships. It is a process where individual needs, abilities, resources, and expectations influence the development of the process and the outcomes.

By any means, research students' supervisors can better benefit from the supervision programs if role models (experienced professors) organize the agenda and share their experiences. For example, professors who have worked as students' supervisors for a long time (15-20 years) could be relevant people to organize programs and inspect supervision sessions. They have been there and should have helpful information to share with other supervisors. Some have some regrets they can disclose to warn the younger (inexperienced) supervisors to benefit learners and families. Others can inform newly employed supervisors how to deal with extraordinary students with diverging, challenging behavior and issues. Therefore, the supervision department, with four main sections, could support teachers and students in dealing with diverse supervision cases.

Each university or municipality may formulate a higher education supervision inspection department. The department could consist of, among others, professors with long experience in teaching and supervision. Academics who have worked with students for at least twenty years could receive a promotion to inspect research students' supervisors and advise them appropriately. In addition, they could deal with the inspection of supervisors in supervision preparation and sessions while communicating with students. Finally, it could reveal students' feedback and how the partners collaborate.

Moreover, they could prepare supervision programs through workshops and seminars for supervisors to teach them how to supervise research students effectively. The experts might also share their supervision experiences with teachers (supervisors) and students while supporting them in acquiring more knowledge and skills for supervision. The department establishment could look like the structure in Figure ten.

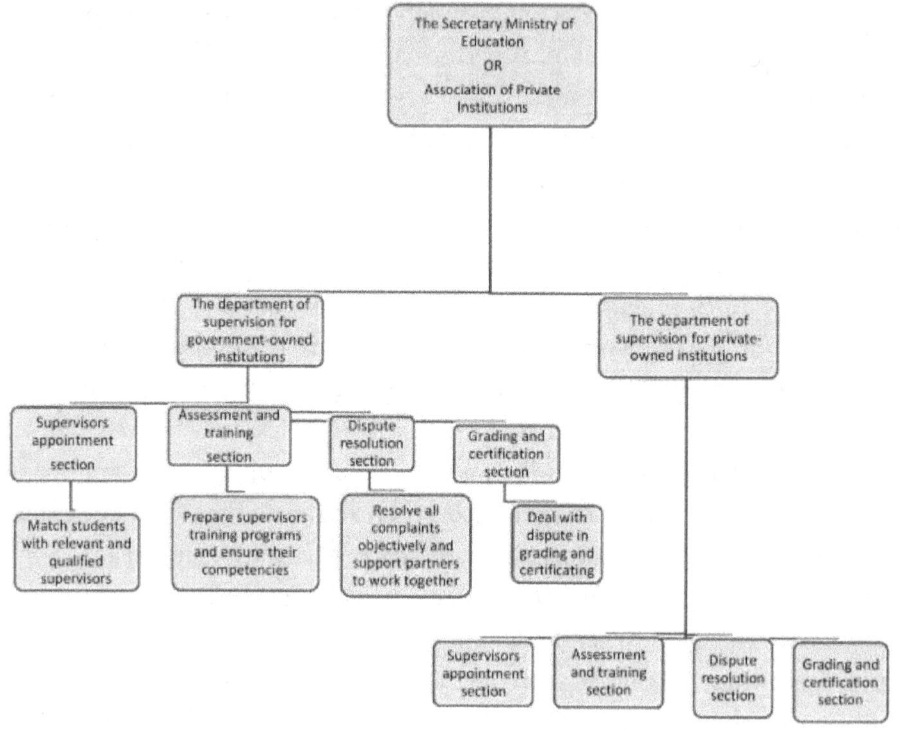

Figure 10. The Department of Supervision, Sections, and Functions

Therefore, Figure ten proposes the sections in the supervision department in higher education. As mentioned earlier, the government-owned institutions and the department could be under the umbrella of the Secretary Ministry of Education. While in private-owned institutions, the department could be under the Association of Private Institutions or another organ and name as agreed contextually. However, both the private and government supervision departments could have four significant sections, thus, the section on supervisors' appointment, the section on assessment and training, the section on dispute and resolution, and the section on grading and certifications.

The supervision appointment, grading, and certifications section could be optional and consist of academics and non-academic experts. In contrast, the other two could consist of only experienced academics, primarily experienced professors. However, regardless of how many sections the department may have, it must be independent. Therefore, the institution it represents should not influence the department's work but collaborate to improve the supervision of research students. Likewise, during the formulation of the department, the institution's leadership should not decide for them. However, the institutional leadership may actively formulate the department and case, considering the optional sections mentioned earlier. Otherwise, the department officials could handle all supervision cases from students' enrolment to graduation.

Of course, this is a general idea, but those who support the mission should re-think critically and formulate a better contextual plan for the department establishment. Moreover, of course, the issue of resources will play a part and may create contextual differences and decide otherwise. However, we cannot expect reduced student attrition if the supervision process is ineffective. The research students should trust their supervisors and institutional management officials when the supervision system is fair and just. Fairness may be created by proposing an independent supervision inspection unit in this book.

8.1.2 Supervision Inspection Unit

Indisputably, it is time to establish a department of supervision to monitor supervisors' practices in higher education. It means that people from the supervision department should oversee supervisors and students in sessions and guide or resolve misunderstandings as early as possible. In addition, it could allow supervision sessions to receive a regular assessment and advice from supervisors' inspectors or experts. The inspectors could evaluate the conduciveness of cooperation between the partners and receive their feedback while advising accordingly. The process could increase partners' knowledge and skills in supervision and maintain an understanding of their expectations. The experts could also support supervisors in identifying students' needs and expectations and strategizing cooperation to achieve their objectives.

Unfortunately, some students obtain supervisors who do not know about their project, creating a challenge to guide them. Hence, the supervision appointment section could match students with supervisors based on the nature of the research project and field knowledge and skills expertise. They could also conduct a background check for the multicultural ability of the supervisors for international students. Awkwardly, searching for the perfect match is not a simple task; it requires commitment and devotion to go through supervisors' qualifications on their academic profiles and social media. Moreover, the section officials could examine supervisors' previous projects and sometimes converse with them.

Supervisors' Appointment Section

Thus, the appointment section should consist of experienced supervisors who could cooperate with non-academic advisors. The main task could be listing and sorting supervisors' qualifications, using all means to obtain authenticity information. For example, teachers sometimes list thousands of capabilities but have only field and research knowledge. The expert could consult different sources to determine the reality of the listed qualifications of the teachers. For example, some teachers write in their profile that they are good at cooperating with students and are ready for criticism, but when students criticize them, they show the other side opposing their display. Sometimes, the official in this section could telephone and converse with the supervisors to clarify their qualifications before matching them with students.

The inspectors assigning supervisors would assess their teachers' qualifications in different dimensions to comprehend the project and students' suitability. For example, some teachers cannot handle multicultural issues and panic when supervising students from other ethnicities. Indeed, although we desire every supervisor to be a multicultural minder and expert, not all can handle some cultural issues without guidance. Therefore, supervisors can be honest with themselves and assign students from the cultures they master than be forced into areas of their weaknesses. On the other hand, forcing a supervisor to supervise students who cannot handle their cultural issues can be risky and may cause dropouts.

Another issue is gender, some supervisors have weaknesses working with students of the opposite sex, and the inspectors could know this and assign them the appropriate students. Although we have read from scholarly literature that supervision functions effectively when the partners have good chemistry, inspectors could match and guide the partners to build the chemistry required. The expert could have studied the supervisors' and students' backgrounds before their connection and helped them communicate their expectations. In this section of the supervisors' assignments, the experts could also deal with the cases related to changing a supervisor when the dispute section proposes. The system of students choosing a supervisor could vanish, and that student would be assigned supervisors based on the assessment conducted by inspectors. The evaluation could examine all the necessary aspects of functional cooperation from academic to non-academic perspectives.

Therefore, six significant issues could determine the matching of a student and supervisor, as indicated in Figure eleven.

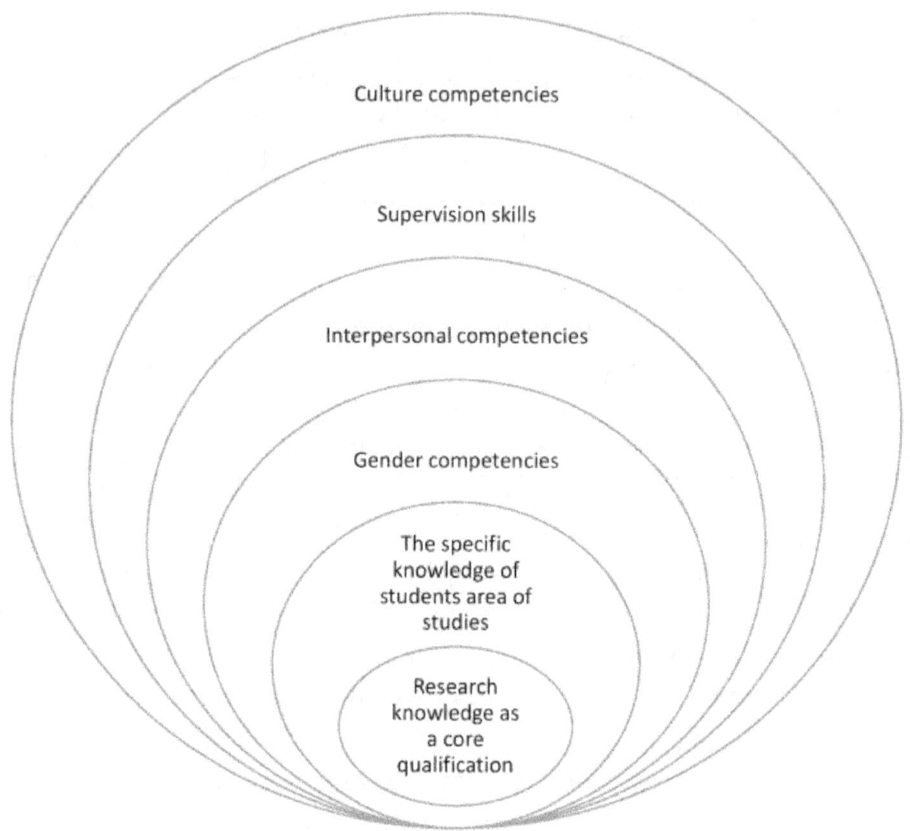

Figure 11. Essential Supervisors' Qualifications

Figure eleven shows the primary qualifications a supervisor should have acquired before accepting supervision responsibilities. First, research knowledge is compulsory for all supervisors, followed by disciplinary (specific areas of studies, humanity (psychology, philosophy, sociology, education, etc.), or science (zoology, botany, geology, mathematics, etc.) knowledge. Other qualifications are gender, supervision, interpersonal communication, and culture. These qualifications could be essential to support the experts in the appointment section to match students with the right supervisors.

Assessment and Training

The second section, "the supervision assessment and training," deals with observing supervision sessions. The inspectors could participate in observing supervision sessions or listen to partners' interactions physically or from a distance to comprehend their relationships and compatibility. In addition, they could provide feedback to inform supervisors of their performances, as in the case of school inspectors. Such practices where someone observes the supervision sessions have no intention to undermine the effort and commitment of the supervisors but to strengthen and ensure the quality of the practice. Therefore, the attention could help supervisors prepare for the sessions, remember their agreements, and show interest in students' projects.

Likewise, the section could consist of experts to qualify supervisors through seminars and workshops to guide them on supervision and issues to be aware of and emphasize. The expert could formulate a procedure with the main points to observe when holding supervision meetings. For example, supervisors could learn how to communicate with students, identify their needs and expectations, and strategize to fulfill them. In addition, students' and teachers' roles could be contextualized by the section's officials and discussed by partners to avoid assumptions that often lead to misunderstandings.

The supervisors could also learn how to deal with complex relationships in supervision and multicultural issues. Experts could discuss all the information concerning students' and supervisors' well-being in this section. The section with experienced professors could inform supervisors of challenges in different relational situations. Besides, supervisors could have an opportunity to discuss in groups some challenges and learn from each other.

Consequently, the inspectors in this section would be responsible for supervisors' qualifications and ensure that all have the necessary knowledge and skills required for supervision. In addition, they could ensure that supervisors are not overloaded with duties and not influenced by external political and religious forces to the extent of not fulfilling students' anticipations. Likewise, the officials could conduct seminars, workshops, and other programs for supervisors to develop and enhance their supervision standards. Some newly appointed supervisors could be required to attend compulsory programs before engaging in supervision.

Finally, the section could deal with institutional and governmental policies that affect students learning and supervision. For example, implementing massification in higher education has led to the increasing number of students a supervisor should supervise. Conversely, the more the university accommodates many students, the more the supervisors' duties increase. Therefore, the section officials could monitor the institution's capacity with supervisors' availability and other resources before allowing students' enrolment.

Likewise, another example of the policy the section official could deal with is students' timely degree completion. Scholars have informed that this policy has created stress and anxiety in supervision. The officials in this section could formulate implementation strategies and support teachers and students accordingly. Indeed, it seems that the policy has not received adequate expert evaluation (I do not want to discuss the procedure itself, but I am giving an example of how supervision experts can hinder negative policy implementation). Consequently, the officials could investigate how the approach benefits students' learning and facilitates supervision. For instance, if the experts discover that the policy hinders the institutional, departmental, and student learning objectives, they could have the power to stop its implementation.

Dispute Resolution Section

The third section, dispute resolution, could deal with conflicts, misunderstandings, and disagreements between the supervision partners. Thus, when a student or supervisor fails to resolve misunderstandings or conflicts, they could send the case to experts in this section. The experts could investigate the claims and support partners in finding solutions, not necessarily changing partners. For this matter, the department could deal with difficulties in supervision, and the expert could make necessary follow-ups to guide students and supervisors to avoid dropouts. For example, the student's email, which I discussed earlier concerning supervision complaints, could be directed to this section in the inspection unit. So, Jackeline and her supervisors could obtain expert advice, and she could probably continue with her studies.

Whether by meetings, exchanging letters, emails, conversation through the telephone, or any other means, the experts could support partners in finding solutions. If necessary, the section could be responsible for all types of disputes, including sexual harassment, before a court of law, if that is necessary. The section could consist of professors from different disciplines, including lawyers who comprehend the institutional and community rules and procedures required for supervision and appropriate interaction between teachers and students.

In case of dispute, the partners could decide whether changing supervisors is the best option or continuing with the same partnership under expert guidance could work. The focus could shift from changing supervisors to equipping supervisors and students with the knowledge and skills required to collaborate in supervision. In most cases, the disputes in supervision are partly due to teachers' and students' lack of supervision skills. I have written a book about it, thus, "The Skills Required of Students to Effectively Collaborate with Academic Supervisors."

Grading and Certifying Section

In the fourth section, the section for grading and certifying, the experts could deal with students' academic assessments, grading, and certifying. In addition, the section experts could deal with complaints about assessment and grading and assign examiners to students' thesis evaluation and oral examinations (where applicable). Fortunately, some universities invite external examiners for the summative evaluation, and students can propose teachers they desire to be part of their examination committee. Therefore, experts in this section of grading and certifying could consider such communications, proposals, and decisions. On the other hand, the experts could deal with students' complaints about assessment and grading fairly.

Similarly, this section of the supervision inspection department could also look at certifying qualified students. For example, some students perform extra-ordinary in many areas of their studies and obtain rewards. Therefore, the section could identify talented students and arrange programs for them to avoid dropping out. Indeed, some students drop out because they realize the quality of learning is lower than expected and do not see the point of wasting their time, hence dropping out. Thus, officials in this section could process challenging programs based on students' abilities, award those talented, and reward students according to their performances. The unit could also ensure the students graduate with the required and expected knowledge and skills and not otherwise.

I heard of the person who applied for a job using someone else certificate and how it was discovered by using graduation photos. This is the story; one graduate employer needed someone to handle a specific assignment in his company. He wanted someone with the same qualifications as himself, someone he could discuss business issues together, so he advertised the position. Many people applied, but he was interested in one applicant whose certificate was from the same year and university he graduated from. The employer was excited and went to his graduation photo to recognize the person but in vain. Thus, he still had a list of his mates, and they collaborated on several projects that made them know each other well.

Nevertheless, it was a compelling case that led him to invite the job applicant to an interview to converse and probably discuss their university experiences. In their conversation, the employer revealed that the applicant had either bought or stolen the certificate of one of his peers. Furthermore, due to the conversation and the questions the applicant obtained, it was revealed that he had never been to the same university. Finally, the discussion led to legal procedures against the applicant to determine where he obtained the certificate.

So, there is a need for certificate scrutinization and ensuring no forgeries made online and paper certificates. Besides, with increased science and technology, universities should formulate strategies to combat grading and certificate forgeries. Thus, the section on grades and certification could ensure that all graduates leave memories at the university that can be proof of their learning apart from making certificates with photos.

Another issue could be dealing with mistakes in certificates. For example, a graduate may find errors in his certificate; the names may spell wrongly and need correction; other times, the grades agreed by the supervisors and the ones on the certificates may differ, needing amendment. Sometimes, it may be the learning contents, where a student has taken courses from different departments that do not appear on the certificate, hence correction. Likewise, the exchange of documents may occur, and sometimes a student may receive grades and certificates that belong to another candidate (address mistakes, identity errors, or sending and the like).

In some cases, students receive certificates lacking the signatures of one or all officials; even for those signing electronically, some mistakes may appear. Different human errors may happen when certifying students that the actors in this section could deal with. The department could accommodate non-academic staff to correct mistakes in collaboration with experts. So, the section's actors could be responsible for dealing with problems associated with grading and certifying.

In summary, we can demonstrate the four mentioned sections in Figure 12

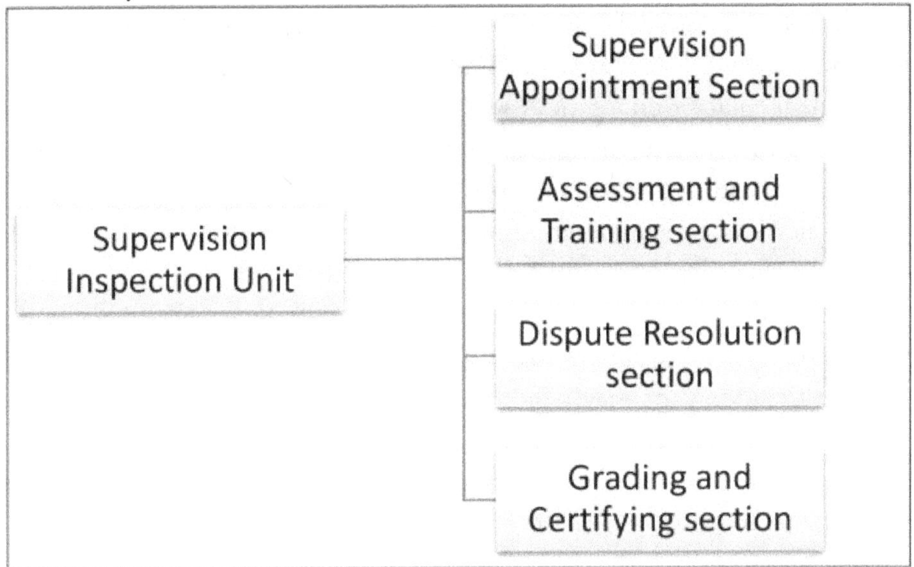

Figure 12. The Proposed Sections in Supervision Inspection Unit

Figure twelve indicates that each institution could have an independent supervision unit. For example, the separate and self-sufficiency department could have four major sections with different responsibilities, as Figure twelve shows. First, the appointment section would be the central section dealing with matching partners. Second, the training section would focus on observing and monitoring supervision sessions and training the partners accordingly. Moreover, the third section would be dispute resolution, where the experts would deal with, among others, challenges in supervision. Finally, the department could have a section for grading and certifying, focusing on examinations, assessments, and certifying students.

Ultimately, all research students could receive information about the department and the sections to consult for different issues, as mentioned. In addition, students could be allowed to communicate with the experts from each section in the orientation programs, where the experts could inform their responsibilities and procedures students need to observe when contacting them. Some details could also be written on the institutions' web pages for students and supervisors to review.

However, to benefit all stakeholders and handle the case reasonably, the inspection unit must be neutral and independent without affiliation with institution leadership or teachers. For example, figure twelve indicates that the department could be under the Secretary Ministry of Education for government-owned institutions. While for private-owned institutions, the department could be under the Association of Private Institutions. If this is not applicable, the department should be under the independent quality control department, not the institutional owner or head.

Nonetheless, as I mentioned earlier, the first and fourth sections of the supervision department could be optional because some university officials may carry most duties mentioned in these sections. For instance, universities worldwide deal with appointing supervision to supervision responsibilities though they do not have professional matches between students and supervisors as required. Therefore, universities may be more professional and realistic in pairing students with supervisors and avoiding the section altogether. The section on grading and certifying can also be optional because all universities perform the duty, although there are some challenges, including biases in grading students. For example, I mentioned Luciferic students who sometimes apply diverse strategies to acquire grades they do not deserve.

Furthermore, grading is a process that needs integrity, and students and other stakeholders must trust the supervisors for this task. So, supervisors need to be trustworthy and comprehend the importance of grading to students, employers, and society. To grade students should not be a simple task; it is not a process of choosing an alphabet to put on their work, but a process of judgment accompanied by honesty, integrity, and accepting responsibility and the consequences. Therefore, the supervision section could investigate the system and criteria for grading students and regulate them according to contextual and international needs.

For example, the section could do something if employers inform weaknesses in grading and the candidates' grades do not align with their abilities. The experts could support examiners, assessors, and supervisors with knowledge and skills to assess and help them perform their tasks objectively and effectively.

Nevertheless, the fairness of the learning process is a vital aspect of establishing the supervision inspection department. Therefore, each university should observe, learn its supervision system, and evaluate the current practices and needs before selecting the department. Furthermore, I firmly believe that student attrition needs attention and that supervision is the primary area to look at. Therefore, establishing the discussed independent supervision inspection unit can minimize and eradicate the challenge.

My Expectation

After receiving your experience with postsecondary teachers, suggestions, and comments on supervision inspection, I will write more on the topic.

Sometimes peoples' experiences may be useful for others to learn. You may write me your experiences with supervisors and whether you wish they had experts to advise and oversee them.

Remember, you have managed to read and benefit from this book because individuals you read about have agreed to share their experiences concerning higher education learning.

So, please tell us your story, and we will air it for others to learn from.

Write to; information.ekambee@gmail.com

Conclusion

Teaching is a rewarding call for those who understand their roles and responsibilities. It is a peculiar and complex career, and not every person can manage and perform teaching in the formal education system. The complexity exists because the duty of a competent teacher is beyond what job descriptions may convey. Even though teaching eliminates learners' ignorance, the teacher should know students' needs and expectations, and the learner must be willing to learn. Understanding learners' needs and expectations is the central road map for the teachers' profession.

Further, the strategizing learning process depends on how the teacher and the learner perceive the needs and expectations and their commitment to meeting them. So, without comprehending these two aspects (needs and expectations) and communicating the strategies, the partners cannot cooperate, and the ignorance problem remains unsolved. For ages, effective learning and teaching processes need a third person to guide, monitor, and evaluate the cooperation between teachers and learners. Unfortunately, in postsecondary education, teachers lack guidance and monitoring of their work, which has been a problem and one reason for student attrition.

Indeed, learning in tertiary education and research training depends on the effectiveness of the supervision process. Traditionally teachers are known for their commitment and passion for learners' success, and the myth has shadowed their need for guidance. However, the change in structure and practices in higher education has created challenges in supervision that call for advice and monitoring of teachers' duties. In addition, some faculties have demonstrated their frustration working with students, indicating career difficulties. Student attrition has also become a topic of interest for scholars, and most institutions suffer from it, showing students' dissatisfaction.

Therefore, establishing a supervision-inspection unit to support supervisors and students in supervision is valid and on time. Furthermore, teachers should obtain expert guidance and support from experienced supervisors who will be inspectors. Indeed, the primary and secondary levels of the formal education system still embrace the work of inspectors in guiding teachers and ensuring the quality of learning. However, in higher education, supervisors who are research students' teachers have no one to guide and challenge their practice objectively. Research students obtain at least two supervisors to guide and cooperate in performing research activities within a limited time. Unfortunately, the supervisors are sometimes busy with other duties; some are not qualified and have no skills to create a conducive learning environment for their students. As a result, students encounter challenges without support from university officials or other neutral and independent persons. Most officials think the solution to the supervision challenge is for complainers to withdraw from the university or change their supervisors. The practice is one of the reasons for the increase in student attrition in higher education worldwide. In some universities, half of the students commence their degrees drop, and others delay completing their degrees partly due to supervision challenges.

The author believes student attrition is not the desire of university stakeholders (students, teachers, parents, governments, institutions, employers, and donor agencies) and that a sustainable solution is needed to combat the problem. Therefore, based on different stakeholders' explanations and the literature, the author proposes that each university establish a supervision inspection department to work with other cases. She introduces a model for the supervision department with four sections; thus, the appointment section, the assessment and training section, the dispute resolution sub-unit, and the grading and certifying division that will play and carry different roles and responsibilities. The units may increase or decrease based on the contextual evaluation of needs and resources in tertiary education.

However, for higher education to comprehend the advantages of the supervision inspection department unit, the author discusses school inspection practices in lower levels of education. She describes the evolution from school inspection to supervision and self-evaluation applied in many schools in different countries. The author discusses the two modes of assessment; thus, visitation and self-evaluation, aimed at monitoring and evaluating teaching and learning effectiveness.

The author informs the role of teachers and the aspects that determine teachers' responsibilities. Elizabeth reminds people of the old days of school inspections and how teachers demonstrated the dedication and devotion required for learners' success. However, she warns people of the danger of joining the teaching profession without a passion for learners' success. She also guides students to mind contextual perception of teachers' duties and to avoid transferring the roles of teachers from one context to another, as it may create misconceptions, misunderstandings, and dissatisfactions.

Therefore, Elizabeth discusses how students can recognize the contextual role of teachers and the determinant of the roles and responsibilities, such as resources and information availability and accessibility, the nature of students' projects, students' ability, and the time allocated for the studies. The author supports readers in comprehending teachers' roles by encouraging them to review university documents and communicate with academic advisors and supervisors. In addition, the students can examine the influence and contributions of supervisors in the institution and community. Finally, they should evaluate their teachers' commitment to their projects and whether they are interested in students' success.

The book explains current student supervision practices in most universities and how officials silence the students' complaints to protect supervisors. The officials have ready-made responses to students' complaints (change the supervisor or leave), and most of the time, students do not receive fair judgment in supervision disputes. The author discusses a case of a doctoral degree student who was encouraged to drop her studies after she filed a complaint. The doctoral student's case and other narratives from higher education stakeholders have become evidence of the biases in higher education when disputes occur between a student and supervisors. Thus, the current practice favors supervisors and students remaining disadvantaged, strengthening the proposal to establish an independent supervision inspection unit.

Ultimately, the book's central argument is encouraging universities to establish an independent supervision inspection unit to eliminate student attrition. However, the book informs the possibility of omitting or adding some proposed sections to suit contextual needs. Indeed, adjustment is needed to ensure the sections provide supervision guidance service with integrity and trustworthiness. Nevertheless, the primary motive for the proposal to establish a supervision inspection department is to allow students and supervisors to obtain expert guidance while monitoring and evaluating the supervisors' practices. Likewise, the department's practices may increase awareness of the contextual role of teachers and students to influence their cooperation and eliminate assumptions that dominate current supervisors' duties.

The officials in the inspection department would also examine institutional and governmental policies and how they affect students' supervision. Their investigation may support policymakers in regulating the already established policies. Again, the author provides an example of two significant policies that have become challenging in higher education. Thus, the policy of massification and students' timely completion of their degrees. Unfortunately, implementing new policies in some tertiary education institutions often does not receive adequate scrutiny and evaluation. As a result, implementing the mentioned policies has caused several unexpected challenges in student supervision that scholars are concerned about and debate. Indeed, the policy influences teachers' task performance and relationship with students in supervision and is part of the student attrition problem. Therefore, establishing the discussed supervision inspection independent department can solve diverse supervision problems, hence students' retention and graduation.

Information is power.

So, the student attrition problem is partly rooted in the challenges that occur in supervision. Therefore, establishing an independent inspection unit to monitor and evaluate supervisors' practices can be part of the solutions required to eliminate the problem.

NOTE

The author has acquired permission to share the stories provided by the informants. She also obtained written documents to use the emails from the department head and the doctoral student.

The names of informants are not the ones written in this book, meaning the ones mentioned are not real, and if a story collides with a real name should be considered a positive coincidence.

Looking forward to your contribution to writing chapter nine (IX)

Thank you.

Reference

Becker, F., & Becker, S. (2008). Young adult carers in the UK. *Experiences, needs, and services for carers aged* 16-24.

Beer, C., & Lawson, C. (2018). Framing attrition in higher education: A complex problem. *Journal of Further and Higher Education*, *42*(4), 497-508.

Bokana, K. G. (2010). The attrition crisis in South African universities. How to keep students on the graduation path. Journal of Interdisciplinary Economics, 22(3), 181–201. https://doi.org/10.1177/02601079X10002200302.

Brimblecombe, N., Ormston, M., & Shaw, M. (1995). Teachers' perceptions of school inspection: A stressful experience. *Cambridge Journal of Education*, *25* (1), 53-61.

Burke, P., & Krey, R. D. (2005). *Supervision: A guide to instructional leadership.* Charles C Thomas Publisher.

Cahn, S. M. (Ed.). (2021). Moral problems in higher education. Wipf and Stock Publishers.

Chapman, C. (2001). Changing classrooms through inspection. *School Leadership & Management*, *21*(1), 59-73.

Chen, Y., & Hoshower, L. B. (2003). Student evaluation of teaching effectiveness: An assessment of student perception and motivation. *Assessment & evaluation in higher education*, *28* (1), 71-88.

Clarke, H. (2021). Sexual harassment in higher education: A feminist poststructuralist approach. University of Derby (United Kingdom).Courtney, S. J. (2016). Post-panopticism and school inspection in England. *British*

Journal of Sociology of Education, 37(4), 623-642.

Cusack, B. O. (1992). An end to school inspection: The New Zealand

experience. *Management in Education, 6*(2), 6-8.

Darwin, S. (2017). What contemporary work are student ratings actually doing in higher education? *Studies in Educational Evaluation, 54*, 13-21.

De Grauwe, A. (2007). Transforming school supervision into a tool for quality improvement. *International Review of Education/Internationale Zeitschrift für Erziehungswissenschaft/Revue Internationale de l'Education, 53*(5/6), 709-714.

Demetriou, C., & Schmitz-Sciborski, A. (2011, November). Integration, motivation, strengths and optimism: Retention theories past, present and future. In *Proceedings of the 7th National Symposium on student retention* (Vol. 201).

Ehren, M. C., Gustafsson, J. E., Altrichter, H., Skedsmo, G., Kemethofer, D., & Huber, S. G. (2015). Comparing effects and side effects of different school inspection systems across Europe. *Comparative Education, 51* (3), 375-400.

Faulkner, S. L., & Adams, T. E. (2021). YouToo: Notes on sexual harassment and assault in the academy. International Review of Qualitative Research, 1940844721991085.

Fearon, D. R. (1889). *School inspection*. Macmillan and Company.

Fisher, R. F., & Engemann, J. (2009). Factors affecting attrition at a Canadian college.

Ford, M. (2018). The Cruelty of Executing the Sick and Elderly: Two Controversial Cases in Alabama Reveal a Disturbing Trend in the Death Penalty in America. *Sup. Ct. Preview*, 186.

Gabb, R., Milne, L., & Cao, L. (2006). Understanding attrition and improving transition. *A Review*.

Gardner, S. K. (2009). Student and faculty attributions of attrition in high and low-completing doctoral programs in the United States. *Higher Education, 58*(1), 97-112.

Golde, C. M. (2000). Should I stay or should I go? Student descriptions of the doctoral attrition process. *The review of higher education, 23*(2), 199-227.

Golde, C. M. (2005). The role of the department and discipline in doctoral student attrition: Lessons from four departments. *The Journal of Higher Education, 76*(6), 669-700.

Grant, B. M. (2005). Fighting for space in supervision: Fantasies, fairytales, fictions and fallacies. *International Journal of Qualitative Studies in Education, 18* (3), 337-354. doi:10.1080/09518390500082483.

Grant. B. M. (2008). Agonistic struggle: Master-slave dialogues in humanities supervision. *Arts and Humanities in Higher Education, 7* (1), 9-27.

Grant, B., & Manathunga, C. (2011). Supervision and cultural difference: Rethinking institutional pedagogies. *Innovations in Education and Teaching International, 48* (4), 351-354. doi:10.1080/14703297.2011.617084

Grant, B., & Pearson, M. (2007). Approaches to doctoral supervision in Australia and Aotearoa, New Zealand. *Supervising Doctorates Downunder: Keys to Effective Supervision in Australia and New Zealand,* 11-18.

Greimel-Fuhrmann, B., & Geyer, A. (2003). Students' evaluation of teachers and instructional quality--Analysis of relevant factors based on empirical evaluation research. *Assessment & Evaluation in Higher Education, 28* (3), 229-238.

Hall, J. B. (2017). Examining school inspectors and education directors within the organisation of school inspection policy: perceptions and views. *Scandinavian Journal of Educational Research, 61*(1), 112-126.

Herman, C. (2011). Obstacles to success-doctoral student attrition in South Africa. *Perspectives in Education, 29*(1), 40-52.

Hillman, N. W., Tandberg, D. A., & Fryar, A. H. (2015). Evaluating the impacts of "new" performance funding in higher education. *Educational Evaluation and Policy Analysis, 37* (4), 501-519. doi:10.3102/0162373714560224

HEFCE (2005). Annual report and accounts in the UK. The Higher Education Funding Council for England.

Husbands, C. T., & Fosh, P. (1993). Students' evaluation of teaching in higher education: experiences from four European countries and some implications of the practice. *Assessment and evaluation in higher education, 18* (2), 95-114.

Johnes, G., & McNabb, R. (2004). Never give up on the good times: student attrition in the UK. *Oxford Bulletin of Economics and Statistics, 66*(1), 23-47.

Karami, A., Spinel, M. Y., White, C. N., Ford, K., & Swan, S. (2021). A Systematic Literature Review of Sexual Harassment Studies with Text Mining. *Sustainability, 13*(12), 6589.

Kaur, A., Kumar, V., & Noman, M. (2021). Partnering with doctoral students in research supervision: opportunities and challenges. *Higher Education Research & Development*, 1-15.

Kemethofer, D., Gustafsson, J. E., & Altrichter, H. (2017). Comparing effects of school inspections in Sweden and Austria. *Educational Assessment, Evaluation and Accountability, 29*(4), 319-337.

Kettell, L. (2020). Young adult carers in higher education: the motivations, barriers and challenges involved–a UK study. *Journal of Further and Higher Education, 44*(1), 100-112.

Kimani, E. N. (2014). Challenges in quality control for postgraduate supervision. *International Journal of Humanities Social Sciences and Education, 1* (9), 63-70.

Lee, A. M. (2007). Developing effective supervisors: Concepts of research supervision. *South African Journal of Higher Education, 21*(4), 680-693.

Lee, A., & Manathunga, C. (2010). Teaching as performance. In *Re-positioning university governance and academic work* (pp. 101-114). Brill Sense.

Lillis, K. M. (1992). Improving basic education: preconditions for successful inspection and supervision-implications for training. International Institute for Educational Planning.

López, R. E. (2020). The Unusual Cruelty of Nursing Homes Behind Bars. *Federal Sentencing Reporter*, *32*(5), 264-271.

Lawton D . and Gordon P. (1987) Her Majesty's Inspectorate (London, RKP)

MacBeath, J. (2006). *School inspection & self-evaluation: Working with the new relationship*. Routledge.

Mayo, D. T., Helms, M. M., & Codjoe, H. M. (2004). Reasons to remain in college: A comparison of high school and college students. *International Journal of Educational Management*.

Maher, M., & Macallister, H. (2013). Retention and attrition of students in higher education: Challenges in modern times to what works. *Higher Education Studies*, *3* (2), 62-73. doi:10.5539/hes.v 3n2p62

Manathunga, C. (2013). Culture as a place of thought: Supervising diverse candidates. In *Of other thoughts: Non-traditional ways to the doctorate* (pp. 67-82). Brill Sense.

Manathunga, C. (2005). The development of research supervision: "Turning the light on a private space." *International Journal for Academic Development*, *10* (1), 17-30.

Manathunga, C. (2017). Intercultural doctoral supervision: The centrality of place, time and other forms of knowledge. *Arts and Humanities in Higher Education*, *16* (1), 113-124.

Manathunga, C. (2010). Intercultural postgraduate supervision: Post-colonial explorations and reflections on Southern positionings. *New Zealand Annual Review of Education, 20*, 5-23.

Marginson, S., & van der Wende, M. (2009). Europeanisation, international rankings

and faculty mobility: Three cases in higher education globalisation. *Higher Education to 2030*, 109.

Marzano, R. J., Frontier, T., & Livingston, D. (2011). *Effective supervision: Supporting the art and science of teaching*. Google: Ascd.

O'Keeffe, P. (2013). A sense of belonging: Improving student retention. *College Student Journal, 47* (4), 605-613.

Papatsiba, V. (2006). Making higher education more European through student mobility? revisiting EU initiatives in the context of the bologna process. *Comparative Education, 42* (1), 93-111.

Pyhältö, K., & Keskinen, J. (2012). Exploring the fit between doctoral students' and supervisors' perceptions of resources and challenges vis-à-vis the doctoral journey. *International Journal of doctoral studies*.

Rivers, I., & Duncan, N. (Eds.). (2013). *Bullying: Experiences and discourses of sexuality and gender*. Routledge.

Saroyan, A., & Amundsen, C. (2001). Evaluating university teaching: Time to take stock. *Assessment & evaluation in higher education, 26* (4), 341-353.

Sempik, J., & Becker, S. (2013). *Young adult carers at school: Experiences and perceptions of caring and education*. London: Carers Trust.

Sempik, J., & Becker, S. (2014). *Young adult carers at college and university.* London: Carers Trust.

Spooren, P., Mortelmans, D., & Denekens, J. (2007). Student evaluation of teaching quality in higher education: development of an instrument based on 10 Likert scales. *Assessment & Evaluation in Higher Education, 32* (6), 667-679.

Spooren, P., Brockx, B., & Mortelmans, D. (2013). On the validity of student evaluation of teaching: The state of the art. *Review of Educational Research, 83* (4), 598-642.

Thomas, G. (1998). A brief history of the genesis of the new schools' inspection system. *British Journal of Educational Studies, 46*(4), 415-427.

Urassa, E.P. (2021). The Principles that Facilitate Successful and Timely Degree Completion. Xlibris Publisher, USA.

Urassa, E. P. (2021). The Cultural Qualities You Must Acquire to Succeed in Higher Education. Xlibris Publisher, USA.

Van der Wende, M. (2007). Internationalization of higher education in the OECD countries: Challenges and opportunities for the coming decade. *Journal of Studies in International Education, 11* (3-4), 274-289.

Van Der Wende, M. (2015). International academic mobility: Towards a concentration of the minds in Europe. *European Review, 23* (S1), S70-S88.

Wadesango, N., & Machingambi, S. (2011). Postgraduate students' experiences with research supervisors. *Journal of Sociology and Social Anthropology, 2* (1), 31-37.

Winchester-Seeto, T., Homewood, J., Thogersen, J., Jacenyik-Trawoger, C., Manathunga, C., Reid, A., & Holbrook, A. (2014). Doctoral supervision in a cross-cultural context: Issues affecting supervisors and candidates. *Higher Education Research & Development, 33* (3), 610-626.

Wisker, G. (2005). *The good supervisor: Supervising postgraduate and undergraduate research for doctoral theses and dissertations.* New York: Macmillan.

Wood, L., Hoefer, S., Kammer-Kerwick, M., Parra-Cardona, J. R., & Busch-Armendariz, N. (2021). Sexual harassment at institutions of higher education: Prevalence, risk, and extent. Journal of interpersonal violence, 36(9-10), 4520-4544.

Yousefi, A., Bazrafkan, L., & Yamani, N. (2015). A qualitative inquiry into the challenges and complexities of research supervision: viewpoints of postgraduate students and faculty members. *Journal of advances in medical education & professionalism, 3* (3), 91.

Zulu, W. V., & Mutereko, S. (2020). Exploring the Causes of Student Attrition in South African TVET Colleges: A Case of One KwaZulu-Natal Technical and Vocational Education and Training College. *Interchange, 51*(4), 385-407.

Index

D

F

G

H

I

T

Thank you

[1] The education system existed before the second World war emphasizing philosophy, history and mathematics for the children of wealthy and powerful people in most societies. The education which was not available for children of families with lower economic and social status. The education which considered and consisted of hierarchical leadership of teachers and encouraged the segregation between educated and non-educated citizens.

[2] The system of education that open for all, and in higher education it allows accessibility to everyone who meet the requirements for admission regardless of their bckgrounds. It encourages higher education for all and the institutions accommodate students across the national and international bourders in different discipline contrary to the elite.

[3] A system of transferring of authority and decision-making responsibilities near to the school stakeholders and empowering them to influence the process and the outcomes of inspection.

[4] *According to Becker and Becker (2008), these are students aged 16-24*

Did you love *A Call for Inspection Unit for Research Students' Supervision*?
Then you should read *The Academic Support Research Students Must Obtain
from Supervisors*[1] by Elizabeth Paradiso Urassa!

The academic Support

Research Students Must Obtain

From Supervisors

Elizabeth Paradiso Urassa

Eka Mbee

2

It is hard to keep silent when higher education students drop out of their
studies every semester. Scholarly literature has indicated that almost fifty
percent of students who commence higher education withdraw. Supervisors do
not comprehend students' needs and expectations, so it has become difficult
for them to strategize how to fulfill student learning goals. As a result, students
drop out because they do not experience support from supervisors in fulfilling
their expectations. Therefore, the author investigated research students'
academic expectations of a competent supervisor and obtained responses
discussed in this book. So, the book is students' voice informing what they
expect academically as a role and responsibilities of a competent supervisor.
Often, supervisors have different roles and responsibilities, but the author

---

1. https://books2read.com/u/mVAlgA

2. https://books2read.com/u/mVAlgA

emphasizes that recognizing, discussing, and fulfilling students' learning expectations should be the priority.

Also by Elizabeth Paradiso Urassa

Strategies to Overcome Challenges in Academic Supervision
Simple and Silly Social -Cultural Strategies to Fight Isolation in Higher Education
The Academic Support Research Students Must Obtain from Supervisors
Articulating Research Students' Relational and Social Expectations
A Call for Inspection Unit for Research Students' Supervision

About the Author

Elizabeth is a former teacher, school inspector, and job advisor. During her Ph.D. study, she recognized students and their learning agency encounter with supervision. Since then, her primary responsibilities have been supporting people, including students and supervisors in higher education, with information and strategies to overcome diverse challenges, including isolation.